I0474303

# Join

# The Money

# Conversation

**Success Is A Personal Thing**

**R NELSON LETSHWENE**

# Join the Money Conversation

—

## Success Is A Personal Thing

Learn the language of money so you can join the money conversation that will free you to create your own financial solutions

*R. Nelson Letshwene*

Published by: Moedi Publishing
PO Box 1766 Rustenburg, 0323 RSA
PO Box 80927 Gaborone, Botswana
**Moedi ISBN: 978-0-9870189-8-4**


**ISBN used on CreateSpace
9781542399890**

"Above all, do not stagnate. Do what you can do within the hour, within the day, within the year. Plan well. But, for God's sake, do not do nothing! For this is not the age of do-nothingness for the chelas of Manjushri and Maitreya and Gautama. This is the age of accelerated doingness"
I AM Manjushri[1]


**Om Ah Ra Pa Tsa Na Dhih**

---

[1] http://encyclopedia.summitlighthouse.org/index.php/Manjushri

DISCLAIMER:

This publication is designed to provide competent and reliable general information regarding the subject matter covered. However, it is published with the understanding that the author and publisher are not engaged in rendering legal, financial, or other professional advice. If legal, financial, or other expert assistance is required, the services of a professional should be sought. The author and publisher specifically disclaim any liability that is incurred from the use or application of the contents of this book.

Nelson Letshwene – PO BOX 80927, Gaborone, Botswana

nelson@moedi.net

# Table of Contents

# READER COMMENTS

Some of the chapters in this book represent some of the material that were covered in my weekly column, Silver Line, which ran in the *Botswana Guardian*. The Silverline column ran from November of 2002 to December of 2013. But the particular material used in this book was between 2004 and 2006.

The following comments are from some of the readers of that column that would write to me from time to time. Their names have been reduced to initials to maintain their privacy, as some of them had requested. Some of their comments have also been edited for clarity. I have put a few of them at the beginning of this book, and some are scattered throughout the rest of the book. Note that where they're placed does not necessarily relate to the chapter preceding, not upcoming. They represented various views based on the many topics that were covered in the newspaper articles, some of which are not necessarily included in this book.

You will also notice that some of the comments have questions. The chapters that follow will be giving answers to many of the questions asked by these readers. Some were general comments, and some were linked to the particular topic covered in a particular week.

### *ARE YOU MONEYWISE?*

*Hey Nelson, I am not so into newspaper reading but I kind of stumbled into your "Silver Line" column and actually read it. Only then did I realise what a dumb and ignorant person I have been "money wise". With money I have never been calm, never! When I have money all I think about is [Shopping malls] ...get my picture...Now after reading your column I can actually get calm with the knowledge that it's my money and no one will take it from me unless I give it away. So, I am learning to budget, been working five years and I have never budgeted before. I've always done impulse buying. All the three cars I've been through were all on impulse. So I am really learning to be calm about money. Ahhh, it's a great feeling really! Knowing you got money in the bank, makes me look good too. Yeah money comes in and finds money... Sweet. I am ready to be peace... Thanks again, M.S.*

**

### *CAN MONEY BUY HAPPINESS?*
*My friend, the topic you covered this week is very interesting but not very easy. Honestly, what matters*

*is the happiness you are talking about. One fact that I know is that money has got a strong meditating effects. Try this, give your Grandma a hundred bucks or even twenty bucks and look at how she is going to change? It will amaze you brother. In short, money can buy happiness. People who are able to buy anything they want are ever happy in the name of money.*

*Look at us ("slaves") to our jobs. When it's month end, you will see how active we are showing signs of happiness. We will get our hard-earned salary and buy everything we want. The only problem is we quickly run out of cash and we start being too low again. If you can get a hundred bucks during this period your happiness revives brother. You do not hide from anything. What do you call that? A person who has got at least enough money to carry his needs has got time to speak to his power of thought and effectively decide his future destiny because he has got peace of mind. Brother I am not talking about the greedy people here. "When the rich think of what car he is going to drive for an outing tonight, another man is thinking of what he is going to eat tonight." So how can he be happy brother? MB        ***

\*\*\*

*I find your articles educational and informative and wish to commend you for a job well done. Hope more 'financially challenged' [citizens] will spare time to read your articles.*

*Regards, K.*

\*\*

# INTRODUCTION

This book is based on a fictional conversation with Robbie Rich, Betsy Broke, and Silver. It is a conversation about personal finances, motivation, and the building blocks of success. They are conversing with an expert in personal finances. The expert simply calls herself **Silver**. She believes every cloud has a silver lining.

Almost everyone will be able to relate to this conversation. There is no financial jargon that cannot be understood by most people. Each topic is discussed through questions and answers. Some of the first few foundational topics are covered without a dialogue.

A conversational approach to our personal finances is often the best way to deal with the issues. Most books and programs are filled with statistics that make most of us feel like failures. You have read the books ... "only 3% will ever make it to the wealthy side, ... or 95% of the population is doomed to failure ..."

If so many of us are doomed to failure, why don't we just get together and talk ...let's have a conversation ... a normal conversation ... no jargon, no statistics, ... just ideas. Sure, we can use the advice of an expert, but let's be free to ask the simple questions and get answers that make sense to us.

# Success Is A Personal Thing

Success is the achievement of a worthy ideal. It is your responsibility to define what a worthy ideal is for you. When you achieve it, are you successful? What creates the greatest stress for people is comparing themselves to others, trying to measure up to others, and in the meantime, losing themselves in the process.

There are currently over seven billion people on this planet and not a single one of them is like you, even if you have an identical twin. There are therefore as many definitions of success as there are individuals on the planet. All you have to do is define yours and be true to it.

While universal standards of success exist because we have agreed about those definitions, it does not mean that you can't adjust those standards to what makes you happy. The goal of life is joy. There is no stress in joy.

Success is literally a personal thing.

*1*

---

# What is my Monthly Payment?

*"There is nothing we receive with so much reluctance as advice."*

Joseph Addison.

**Silver:** Have you ever heard the saying: "The Road to Hell is paved with good intentions"?

**Betsy Broke:** That sounds like a description of my life. Always intending good but ending up in trouble.

**Silver:** How so, tell us more about yourself.

**Betsy Broke:** After graduating from university and seeing a big cheque for the first time, I started thinking, 'I'm rich!'

**Silver:** So, what is the first thing that you did?

**Betsy Broke:** What do you think? I did the most logical thing for someone with lots of money for the first time. I went shopping! I went to the clothing store to get some 'corporate working' clothes. When I got there, I thought I had died and gone to heaven, they told me I could just open an account and pay a little every month, allowing to take more clothes than I actually had money for at the time. I was ready to look the part at work.

**Silver Line:** So, then you thought that your money could go so much further if you only had to pay small monthly instalments?

**Betsy Broke:** Of course! I don't have to think about buying anything with lump sums. And what do you know? Word gets around. My entire extended family finds out that I am employed, so they start placing their orders.

**Silver:** And of course, you indulged them.

**Betsy Broke:** You know me with my golden heart. I love everyone so I indulged them for a while, buying groceries, and clothing my siblings, nieces, and nephews. Now they think that this money grows on trees. The orders don't come to an end. After a while I started feeling that I'm not getting anywhere. I've been working for several years and have not made any progress.

**Silver**: What did you do then?

**Betsy Broke**: Well, I decided it's time to move out! I got an apartment and suddenly I felt free! … For the first month.

**Silver**: Just one month?

**Betsy Broke**: Well, one problem is, the apartment needed some furniture. So, I went to the furniture store and opened an account and since the monthly payment was affordable, I took extra pots and plates and a few more things to make my place look nice and homely.

**Silver**: Free at last?

**Betsy Broke**: I looked at my pay slip and my bank account, and realised that this new item called rent is taking a lot of money from me. After paying rent, food, utilities, the telephone, entertainment, my store accounts, and that contribution I intended to make to my mother at home every month … this picture was not so rosy any more. I intended to buy a car but with this pay slip, it was not going to happen any time soon.

**Silver**: So?

**Betsy Broke:** Well, getting a car loan or personal loan was one way …

**Silver**: Did you think about "Total Cost of ownership?"

**Betsy Broke**: What is that?

**Silver**: The instalments for the car plus fuel, plus insurance, plus maintenance costs …

**Betsy Broke**: Well I didn't think about the other things but I did think about the instalments, and I realised that they would add more burden to my pay at the end of each month.

**Silver:** So, you didn't get the car.

**Betsy Broke:** I didn't get the car but I got something else.

**Silver**: I'm curious?

**Betsy Broke:** Well, it's not like I was trying to get something else, but I thought about inviting a friend to come and stay with me so we can share the bills. Jane was looking to move out of her mother's home. So, I discussed this with my boyfriend, and guess what? He was thinking about moving out of his parents' home also.

**Silver:** So, you were spoilt for choice?

**Betsy Broke**: Well, it's as much a financial decision as it is a social decision.

Let's fast forward:

So, after sorting out the social conundrum, her boyfriend Robbie Rich moved in. They had good future intentions. His salary plus her salary plus his car and other things would be helpful. They partied and had a good time, except Betsy's family, they were not happy that she was not helping them out anymore.

Betsy and Robbie's solution? Let's get married! The family would understand why she would not be able to help them. It's family matters. So, they got married.

A few months later she came home to Robby and said: "guess what honey? We're going to have a … baby!"

One day they woke up, and it did seem like one day, the baby needed school uniform, school fees, cool clothes, and suddenly, a cell phone and a tablet!

Now they need another car because this one old and is not enough anymore. They are in debt up to their eyebrows.

Now they are in their late thirties, with two kids and old furniture that needs replacing, and eventually they realised how much rent they'd been paying all these years. They could have paid off their own home by now! So, they bought a house while they still could, and … pay-cheque-to-pay-cheque survival … Life goes on. Credit cards are maxed. Clothing accounts demand attention. Hire purchase contracts require regular instalments. The house needs some maintenance. And the children are growing …

**What can they do?**

They have a choice; life can continue as it is all the way to their middle ages while they exist in the middle class, or they can make decisions to take control and learn something about money … about their personal finances …

And so, they invited Silver to come over for a chat

**Robbie Rich**: How did we get here?

**Betsy Broke**: Did we make any financial mistakes along the way?

**Robbie Rich**: Everything seemed so normal. I mean, we are not extravagant people. How come we're always broke before even month-end?

**Betsy Broke**: We struggle to reach month end, but as soon as the month is over, so is the money.

**Silver**: Yes, you made some mistakes, but it can hardly be your fault!

**Robbie Rich**: How can my mistake not be my fault?

**Silver**: Most people don't know better. Most people don't understand the systems that imprison them. They actually think that some of these systems are set up to help them, whereas they are set up to imprison them.

**Betsy Broke**: What are you talking about?

**Silver**: When it comes to money, most people can't think beyond one month. They are stuck in a monthly system of thinking. They don't even see the years passing by because all they see is the month. They can't even have a one-year plan, let alone three to five years. Their money leaves them in small amounts one month at a time into the pockets of those who have long-term plans for it.

**Robbie Rich**: We need to take some time to talk about this planning thing!

**Silver**: Not before we cover some of our psychology on money!

**Betsy Broke**: Such as?

**Silver**: The Secrecy of money!

# 2

## The Secrecy of Money

*"You are the world. When you transform yourself, the world you live in will also be transformed."*
Deepak Chopra

The trouble with money is that it is invisible! Everyone is playing 'hide-and-seek' with money. They seek, when they find it, they hide it, then it 'disappears', then they are out seeking again, so that when they find it, they can hide it again, only to have it disappear again.

It's a vicious cycle. Nobody wants anybody to know how much they make and what they do with it. Everybody seems to be having problems but nobody can help anybody because no one would talk! Our culture has made money a big secret.

Money is silence!

**Betsy Broke:** Surely there's something we can do about the secrecy of money.

**Silver:** Break the secret code. Break the silence.

**Robbie Rich:** Where do we begin? Surely, I can't just go around telling everybody how much money I have or what my financial problems are.

**Silver:** I don't think it's everybody who needs to know. But surely the people closest to you need to know. We hide money not just from strangers, which may be understandable, but we hide it from our partners and children as well.

**Betsy Broke:** I guess if my children knew my financial situation they would really understand, and stop making undue demands.

**Robbie Rich:** But most parents don't want to disappoint their children, or burden them with financial concerns!

**Betsy Broke:** Yeah, so they make promises, which later prove difficult to fulfil. Either the parents borrow money to try to fulfil these promises, or the children get disappointed.

**Silver:** No one would get disappointed who has no expectation. All our disappointments are a result of expectations. If everyone in the household knew the truth, then there would be no undue expectations, and thus, no disappointments. It is our secret code that is killing us. We have built secrecy around all things that are important to us.

**Betsy Broke:** Around what other important things have we established secrecy?

**Silver:** We have built secrecy around the four cornerstones of the human experience, Money, Love, Sex, and God. We want to love and be loved and yet we hide our feelings about love. We build expectations, which inevitably lead to disappointments. This has caused more trouble in our love relationships, not to say anything about our sexuality – the greatest secret of them all. As for God, we are even embarrassed to admit we believe, but in our secret closets we wail at God, and come out disappointed, waiving our fists to the skies.

**Betsy Broke:** How can we remove the secrecy?

**Silver:** Around money, for instance, let the paperwork come out. Let everyone in the family know the truth. If parents would sit around the table with their children and say, here is what we have, and here is where it is going: rent or mortgage, food, utilities, transport, school fees, etc., they will be teaching their children more about money, than if they keep the secret code.

**Betsy Broke:** That is a great idea. This way children will be learning about budgeting and responsibility, and good management of resources.

**Robbie Rich:** That will surely create fairer expectations and fewer disappointments.

**Silver:** The same can be done about the other things around which we have built a secret code! We have a society filled with dysfunctional sexual practices because we will not openly discuss sex. We will not discuss love, and we certainly do not discuss money.

**Betsy Broke**: So where do we begin?

**Silver**: You start wherever you are.

**Robbie Rich**: You mean if I'm broke I just tell

them I'm broke and here's where we go from here?

**Silver**: Families need leadership in all areas, including finances. Parents need to take the leadership role. A leader assesses the situation and tells everyone what's going on. A leader tells the troops what the plan is and where we're going.

**Robbie Rich**: What if the leader doesn't have a plan?

**Silver**: Then the leader invites everyone so that they can draw the plan together. That plan that has been drawn together has a greater chance of being owned by all and thus carried out than a plan that is being imposed on everyone.

**Betsy Broke**: So we start budgeting together?

**Silver**: That's a start!

## READER COMMENTS

*Hi Nelson, I enjoy reading your articles in the newspaper and I must say they are fantastic, that is the only reason I even buy the newspaper on Fridays. Your articles have helped me to be able to understand money better and create a better attitude when it comes to spending. Keep doing what you know how to do best. Regards, P.U.*

**3**

---

# Is This A Budget Or A Spending Sheet?

*"If you don't change direction, you may end up where you are heading"*
Lao Tzu.

---

**Robbie Rich**: But we are doing the best we know how. We budget every month, but still, things don't fall into place. What is really going on here?

**Silver:** Now you are starting to ask some real questions. The trouble with so many people is that they've never taken the time to understand what proper financial planning is all about. They always assumed they know, until they are in trouble.

**Betsy Broke:** But we're told we should budget

and we're doing it!

**Silver:** Let's talk about that budget that everyone does. At the end of every month, there's that little sheet that comes out called a budget. The biggest trouble is not that people don't want to plan, but the truth is that they don't know what a budget is. They think by writing out an expense sheet every month that they are 'budgeting'.

**Robbie Rich:** Wait a minute. Isn't a budget that very sheet that guides you on how to spend your money?

**Silver:** Let's think bigger. Can you imagine if the government did that? Do you see the Minister of finance looking at how much Value Added Tax (VAT) or Income Tax was collected this month, and then, and only then, deciding what will be paid this month? (Would your salary be covered if you worked for the government – you would wonder!) It's ridiculous. Yet, that's what you do every month. Anyone else?

**Betsy Broke:** But everyone I know does that.

**Silver:** Financial Planning is not necessarily synonymous with budgeting. A *planning budget* must be done at least *once* a year, and it must include two to five year planning in it. What you do every month, is monitoring, not 'budgeting'.

A budget gives you a chance to decide how much money you *want* to make, and what you *want* to save and spend for that year.

**Betsy Broke:** Yes I want more but my employer won't pay more! So I work with what I have …

**Silver:** Listen. A planning budget is not necessarily based on what you already have, but it gives you a chance to grow. A planning budget is not just planning to spend, based on a given amount of money coming in. It should also include <u>planning to earn more</u>.

**Robbie Rich:** You mean getting a new job?

**Silver:** Think of ways of planning to increase your means. What can you do? What are the possibilities? Unless you start thinking about this, you will not come up with anything. Having to write some ideas down in your planning budget will get your creative juices flowing.

This "monthly budgeting" leads to increased frustration because it doesn't work.

**Betsy Broke:** That's why I've been telling Robbie to toss it out the window because it just frustrates me!

**Robbie Rich:** The trouble is we did toss it out and have paid lip service to it. And we went to the loan sharks to borrow survival money. That's why my credit card is maxed to the limit.

**Betsy Broke:** That's why that squeaky bed and ragged sofa have not been replaced yet …

**Silver:** It's because they never made it on the real budget three years ago … because there was no budget … no foresight!

**Robbie Rich:** But these 'affordable' gadgets made it on the spending sheet! We have been living day to day ever since we met.

**Silver:** If you don't change this day-to-day living mentality, this will go on until retirement. You have set yourselves up to fail …

**Betsy Broke:** Okay. I need to breath. What should we really do?

**Silver:** Have you heard of the saying: 'think outside the box'?

**Robbie Rich:** Aaah … so we've been living in the

box of conformity!

**Silver:** First, you should make the *decisions* to change! Once you are *committed* to a decision, you will seek and find help. Reading a personal finance book could be a good decision. Attending a Personal Financial Seminar could be a good place to start. Or you could take a Personal Finance Course. Learning about Personal Financial Management will go a long way in transforming your lives. What you don't know about money will hurt you. Next, let's develop a debt reduction plan and a proper budget.

**Robbie Rich:** So, wait a minute, let me get this right before we continue. Are you saying our monthly budget is wrong?

**Silver:** It is not wrong. It is faulty!

**Betsy Broke**: Same difference to me?

**Silver**: "Wrong" is a statement of judgment. "Faulty" is about functionality. If something is not functional, it may mean that it is broken, but not wrong. This is not a "budget". It is a spending sheet! That's what makes it faulty. It will not accomplish the purpose for which it is supposed to be set up.

**Betsy Broke**: Yes, but it guides us on how to spend what little we have.

**Silver**: It may be doing so, but it's incomplete. And it does not tell you how to increase what little you have. It does not help you to see beyond the one month. It imprisons you to be a "one-month" thinker. It actually cripples your viewpoint.

**Robbie Rich:** Oh, so a real budget would include, not just the spending side, but the plan to increase our income?

**Silver:** Yes. When was the last time you explored your possibilities and opportunities to increase your income?

**Betsy Broke:** All we do is complain about how little we're earning.

**Silver:** Do you want to tell me you don't have other skills and talents that you could explore to increase your income; skills and talents that I would call "lazy", because they remain unemployed even though you have them?

**Robbie Rich:** I suspect you won't accept our excuse that we don't have time?

**Silver:** That is the one department where God has been fair to all. Everyone on our planet, rich or poor, gets a full 24 hours a day. No less, no more! The rich get rich within the same 24-hour cycle that the poor use to get poor.

**Betsy Broke:** But of course, we're not equal and we can't all accomplish the same things.

**Silver:** That is true. But it will also not help you to sit here and argue for your limitations!

**Robbie Rich:** I should identify my limitations and overcome them, instead of strengthening them by defending them?

**Betsy Broke:** So, the difference between a budget and a spending sheet is that a budget includes my untapped talents and skills, and challenges me on how to increase my earning?

**Silver:** Absolutely. That way you can expand your means, instead of struggling for years to fit within your means.

You are a human being, a growing being. Today's needs cannot reasonably be expected to fit into yesterday's means. As you grow, and your family grows, you need to find your own ways of how to grow your means. And don't sit here and think it's your employer's fault for not increasing your income. Your employer will almost always only pay you in accordance with predetermined "market rates".

**Robbie Rich:** It is time to grow!

# 4

# Accounting Leads To Accountability

*"You should treat all debt, good or bad, the same way you treat a loaded gun, and that is, with a lot of respect."*

Robert Kiyosaki.

Our friends are ready to face the music. However, before they can develop a budget and a debt reduction plan, they need to honestly face their financial affairs. An honest accounting of what you have or do not have is the only reasonable place to start, as Robert Kiyosaki, author of *Rich Dad Poor Dad* says: accounting leads to accountability.

Kiyosaki tells that even when he and his wife

were in debt, they still had a twice-monthly audit. The accountant came, books came out, and they faced their financial situation. Facing where you are at honestly, helps you to get a resolve to deal with it. If you hide and lie, you will never know what you are dealing with, and thus will never get the opportunity to resolve the issues.

The devil continues to hide in the closet, but needs regular feeding. And the fatter he gets, the more gluttonous he gets, and the thinner you become, without knowing exactly what's eating you. Then you may fade into insolvency, bankruptcy, or a psychiatrist's couch with depression.

**Betsy Broke:** So, what is the first thing we need to do?

**Silver:** You are already doing it. You are engaged in this conversation. The next thing is not a deed. It is a thought. It is a decision. A decision to change. If your motivation is right, the right deeds will follow. The next thing you guys will need to do is to make some lists.

- The first list is the list of your incomes from all sources.
- The second list is a list of living expenses from month to month up to at least a year. You can start with three months, but you must go towards the full year.
- The third list is a list of all your debts – the names of who you owe and the totals of each debt.
  - Then there must be a list of commitments – this is expected instalments on all debts.
- Then there is the list of assets that you have.

**Robbie Rich:** What is the purpose of making these lists?

**Silver:** This is "the base line". This is what is going on. These lists represent the status quo. Unless you get to know the status quo, you won't be able to know what to change.

With these lists you will be able to build your financial reports – the income and expense report, the balance sheet and you will be able to assess the flow of cash.

(For a comprehensive way to deal with these please refer to the book *The Money Field*[2] by yours truly)

Do not get overwhelmed by any of these lists, especially the list of debts and the list of commitments. Don't get discouraged by the list of incomes and of assets either! Especially if you think it's too small. Just face it.

**Betsy Broke:** This will take some time.

**Silver:** Take all the time you need, but do it. Drawing a functional annual budget is dependent on real information.

Now Betsy Broke and Robbie Rich need to answer the following questions honestly. Join them if you can.[3]

Give yourself a 1 for every time you answer yes:

---

[2] The Money Field – In the Game of Money, All are Players, but Some are More Skilled than Others, by R. Nelson Letshwene, (Moedi Publishing, 2016). Also available on www.amazon.com )

[3] Some of the Question here are from Robert Kiyosaki's book, *Rich Dad's Guide to becoming rich, without cutting up your credit cards* (Time Warner Audio Books, 2003)

1. Do you routinely pay your bills late?
2. Have you hidden a bill from your spouse?
3. Have you bought something recently that you didn't need or couldn't afford?
4. Have you neglected to do regular repairs on the car because of insufficient funds?
5. Do you regularly spend more than your pay-cheque?
6. Have you put off saving money for a rainy day?
7. Have you been turned down for credit?
8. Does your total debt, mortgage excluded, exceed your rainy day reserve?
9. Has your life insurance lapsed because of insufficient funds or lack of payment?
10. Do you receive less than half of your pay-cheque because of direct debits for loans or accounts?

Add up all the numbers. If you have zero, that's great, you may already be in control of your cash flow. (But cash flow control is not necessarily synonymous with financial control.)

If you scored in the 1-5 range, you need to think about reducing your debt to control your cash flow.

If you scored in the 6 –10 range, you may be headed to financial disaster. It's time to act.

### Reader Comments

*Hi! Nelson. I hope you're doing very great. I want to thank you for the wonderful teaching you give us your readers in the Silverline. Thanks a million times! Looking forward to more of your educating tips. W.*

\*\*\*

# 5

## The Planning System!

*"Never spend your money before you have earned it."*
Thomas Jefferson

Now that Robbie Rich and Betsy Broke have faced the hard questions and answered them honestly, they can draw a plan that will help them to recover. The exercises above are very emotional and may take some people some time to deal with and to face the truth. They are however very important, and they need to be done. If you need help in facing your financial situation, then get the help.

The key with a planning system is that it must propel you forward, instead of holding you at the same place or worse, taking you backwards.

Now you must determine the flow of your cash. What happens to money when it arrives into your system? You need to watch it so that you can make decisions and perhaps redirect the flow of your cash if it is going the wrong way.

In the book, **The Money Field**, the flow of cash in people's lives is discussed and illustrated clearly on a template I call "the money field". If you have not read that book, I strongly recommend that you do, or its first edition called *Functional Mastery Over My Finances*.


**Silver:** Let us examine the flow of your cash. What do you observe?

**Betsy Broke:** For me, unfortunately the money does not even arrive into my hands. I hear you talk about systems. Maybe the system is working against me.

**Silver:** What systems have you set up against yourself?

**Betsy Broke:** Okay, my system is set up such that the money goes to others before it even reaches me. My pay-slip shows that the money gets taken from my employer by my creditors and only very little makes it to my bank account, where further debit orders are waiting to dock it before it reaches my pocket.

**Silver:** So you have set it up in such a way that you really have little or no control over the flow of your cash.

**Betsy Broke:** It seems I have given up control by signing it away in my money contracts with others.

**Silver:** This makes it difficult, although not impossible, for you to change your mind.

**Robbie Rich**: For me, whereas my pay-slip shows that I get most of my money from my employer, my bank statement shows that the direct debits and stop orders on my account are like bloodsuckers and I am still broke at the end of the pay period.

**Silver:** Your pay slip and your bank statements are good places to start tracing the flow of cash in your monetary system. Everyone should at least do that.

**Robbie Rich:** So, how do we create the annual budget?

**Silver:** You can use a spreadsheet in your computer or get a notebook and start writing. Just like in the example below, in the top row you fill in all the 12 months of the year, and on the left you fill in your incomes first, and then a list of all your expenses. You will add up your incomes from all sources and you will add up all your expenses for each month. At the end of all the rows are your annual totals for each line item.

At the bottom of each column you will subtract the total expenses for each month from the total income for that month, and you will get either a positive number (surplus), or a negative number (deficit).

At the end of the last row you will know whether you have a positive year or a negative year.

(See next page)

| | Month 1 ... | Month 2 ... | Month 3 ... | ANNUAL TOTAL |
|---|---|---|---|---|
| Income 1 ... | | | | |
| Income 2 ... | | | | |
| **TOTAL INCOME** | | | | |
| Expense 1 ... | | | | |
| Expense 2 ... | | | | |
| Expense 3 ... | | | | |
| **TOTAL EXPENSES** | | | | |
| **SURPLUS/ DEFICIT** | | | | |

**Betsy Broke:** It could be very depressing to know in advance that you are going to have a negative balance at the end of the year.

**Silver:** It is better to know in advance, so that you can make plans, than to be surprised by the amount of debt you are in at the end of a year.

**Robbie Rich:** So, knowing in advance that we will have a negative gives us an opportunity to put more controls in place to avoid the negative?

**Silver**: Right. And finding out you will have a positive allows you to set up a savings and investment plan.

**Betsy Broke:** We could also activate our "lazy" skills and talents to improve our financial life in advance.

**Robbie Rich:** What is the best way to allocate your money?

**Silver:** Allocations will differ from person to person and from family to family according to their situations. You must, however, make some rules that you can live by.

**Robbie Rich:** Rules? Like what?

**Silver:** Yes, rules. Like:

- o "Pay yourself first" rule.
- o Controlled expenditure rule
- o Investment rule
- o Debt management rule
- o Protection Rule

You can make budgetary allocations to fulfil these rules.

**Robbie Rich:** What do you mean?

**Silver:** You can allocate, say 10% of your income

to the "pay yourself first rule". That means every time you get an income, 10% is not available for expenses or anything else because it is set aside towards your own financial investments and financial growth. That is the "pay yourself first rule". You "pay yourself" in order to build your wealth with that money.

**Robbie Rich:** Oh, so, it's not money I'm setting aside to spend later, say on a holiday?

**Silver:** No. A holiday is an expense. It does not build your wealth. The "pay yourself rule" is only about building wealth.

Robbie Rich: So, how does it relate to the "savings rule" or "investment rule"?

**Silver:** Saving can be for an emergency, but investing is for building wealth.

**Robbie Rich:** What about that protection rule?

**Silver:** You can allocate say 5% to protection, which means all your insurances. Protection has to do with risk management.

**Betsy Broke:** But how do you avoid getting into debt?

**Silver:** There are two ways to avoid debt. The

first step is to allocate enough of your current income towards your living expenses, so that you don't have to borrow money to survive at the end of the month. You can allocate say 65% of your income towards your living expenses.

Secondly, you also decide in advance how much of your monthly earnings should go to servicing debt and you work towards that goal if you are already outside that boundary. If you say only 20% should go towards servicing debt, but you find that you are already using 40%, then you work towards your goal over time.

**Robbie Rich:** So, you are saying we should set the ideal allocation, and then contrast it with the reality?

**Silver:** Essentially, yes.

**Robbie Rich:** So, the ideal could be:

- o 10% to saving and investments ("Pay yourself first")
- o 5% to Protection (Insurances)
- o 20% to Debt servicing
- o 65% to living expenses

**Silver:** It will differ from family to family, but yes,

that could be your ideal.

**Betsy Broke:** What if our current situation is far from this ideal?

**Silver:** Remember that your financial life is inextricably intertwined with your real life. To change your financial life you will have to change your practical real life. Every change you make to your finances will affect your real day-to-day life. To reach your ideal plan, you will have to start making adjustments in your real life.

**Betsy Broke:** That is not going to be easy! There are many other people involved in our lives and in our money!

**Silver:** Didn't we agree to break the silence?

**Robbie Rich:** So we will have to break the silence with our creditors, our families, our friends, and our colleagues!

## Reader Comments

*Hi, First let me congratulate you for such a brilliant column. You may not be aware but it's a subject of discussion every weekend in Tlokweng amongst "us"- wannabe rich- guys. What I have found more appealing about this column is the numerical touch to the arguments. You once said a person has to save at least 10% of his salary before thinking of his deductions. I found this quite appealing! But I am at a bit of a loss. What is this saving specifically for? Is it for savings just in case of a desperate need, retrenchment, holiday, retirement... I am asking this because I need to distinguish whether this is for retirement as you seemed to have been implying. I am an upcoming insurance professional and want clarity because I believe one needs to know what he is specifically saving for. More so that one is not allowed to touch this money (annuity). The 10% is a good figure. Are you simply encouraging the culture of saving? T*

**

# 6

---

# The Debt Spiral

*'Neither a borrower nor a lender be'.*
Benjamin Franklin

**Betsy Broke:** Before we go any further, I would really like us to talk briefly about some principles of debt reduction or debt management.

**Robbie Rich:** Yes, that's a good idea. What should our attitude be towards our current debt?

**Silver:** Well, when you're in debt, there's only one-way out: that is to pay it off. Without getting overwhelmed about the fact that you are in debt, you need to make a plan and stick with your plan until you are out.

**Betsy Broke:** I think my problem is that while I'm dealing with what I call big debt, you know, the ones which come out of my payslip or on debit orders from my bank accounts, I get other "small informal" debts along the way, and then I have to focus on paying these off, sometimes at the detriment of the more "formal" debt.

**Silver:** If you want to get out of debt, you need to stop accumulating any debt, regardless of how small. As part of your money rules, you need to make the rule that you will never borrow again.

**Betsy Broke:** Easier said than done!

**Silver:** True that. You need to identify which pockets are easier for you to go back to more frequently. How does your debt accumulate? Is it through cash loans? Is it your credit card? Is it your overdraft facility? Is it store cards? Is it through friends and family?

**Betsy Broke:** For me, all those avenues are available to me and I have used them all interchangeably from time to time.

**Robbie Rich:** For me it's my credit card and my overdraft facility. They actually feed each other. My cheque account pays off my credit card instalments. But my cheque card is where my overdraft facility is. So, I'm essentially using one debt to feed the other.

**Silver:** That is exactly what revolving credit does. More often than not it's when you are paying one debt with another. Robbing Peter to Pay Pau, so to speak.

**Betsy Broke:** Some people say I should just consolidate them. Take one big debt and clear all the others so that I can face only one. What are your thoughts on that approach?

**Silver:** The biggest problem with debt consolidation is that it does not close those other avenues. They remain open. If you don't change your behaviour, you will be right where you started within a year or two.

**Betsy Broke:** But it takes off the pressure by reducing my instalments.

**Silver:** Yes, it's like painkillers. It takes away the pain temporarily but not the source of the problem, and it delays real healing. You will be in debt hospital longer. The one big debt may demand very little from you in terms of current instalments, but it extends the amount of time you will remain in debt. Some "small" debts that could have been paid off within six months are now rolled over into the big one that will take you seventy-two months.

**Robbie Rich:** Six years is a long time to be paying off a loaf of bread that I bought with a credit card.

**Silver:** Yes it is very long indeed. And because the credit card that was "cleared" by your consolidation loan was not closed off, it remains open to tempt you again before long. So does the overdraft facility. So do the informal loans that you have taken before. They're still there, waiting for you to get in financial difficulties again.

**Robbie Rich:** That has happened to me many times.

**Betsy Broke:** So, what's the real solution then?

**Silver:** Well, it's really up to you. Do you want to stay in debt or get out of debt?

**Betsy Broke:** I'd like to get out of course!

**Silver:** Then get out!

**Betsy Broke:** How?

**Silver:** Pay off the people you owe and never

take their money again. Cut down all those avenues that are a trap for you. When one debt is paid off, close off that avenue. Learn to depend only on your own money.

**Betsy Broke**: What if your own money is not enough?

**Silver:** Then make more of your own!

**Robbie Rich:** Can we revisit that list of debt avenues again?

**Silver:** The key there is to identify those avenues. List them as your traps. Be aware that these are your traps. Would you knowingly step onto a trap?

**Betsy Broke:** I think we need to seriously talk about making more money. Where do we start?

(For a more comprehensive debt management plan, refer to the book *The Money Field[4]*)

---

[4] *The Money Field – In the Game of Money, All are Players, but Some are More Skilled than Others*, by R. Nelson Letshwene, (Moedi Publishing, 2016). Also available on www.amazon.com )

## MONEY MATHEMATICS 1[i]

Norman is a super sales person when it comes to bikes. He also sees it as his duty to get everyone on a bike, so he is delighted when a customer comes into his shop and without any hesitation buys a bike for $99. The customer pays for it with a cheque for $150, and as the banks are closed, Norman asks his neighbour to cash it. He returns, gives his customer the change of $51 who then rides off at speed. Calamity follows. The cheque bounces, the neighbour demands his money back, and Norman has to go to a friend to borrow the money. The bike originally cost him $79.

How much did Norman lose altogether? Discuss.

Source: Tony Crilly; 50 Mathematical ideas you really need to know; Quercus,

# 7

## Increase Your Means Not Your Expenses

*"If your outgo exceeds your income, your upkeep is your downfall"*
Unknown

**Betsy Broke**: Getting out of debt, it seems to me, is more than commitment to the plan. It seems to require additional resources. Now that we have this debt reduction plan, how can we speed up our payments?

**Silver**: If you stick to the plan, you will eventually get out of debt. To speed up the payments, you may have to increase your means.

**Robbie Rich**: We did allude to this idea of increasing our means earlier, and I 'm glad we're coming back to it. How do we do that?

**Silver**: There are a number of ways. Getting a pay increase is one way.

**Betsy Broke**: But surely that's not in my control!

**Silver**: On the contrary, there are ways you can influence your employer to give you a pay increase. One of the ways is to make yourself *more* valuable to the organisation, and make sure that they notice.

**Robbie Rich**: How do I do that?

**Silver**: Here are a few suggestions: Learn a new essential skill. Essential to the company you work for. So essential that it will make a difference in the organisation. If they're thinking of hiring a new person, it would easier for them to increase your salary and let you do that job than to hire a new person.

**Robbie Rich:** But how would I know the needed essential skill?

**Silver:** Pay attention to what's going on in the organisation. Sometimes you see yourself struggling with certain duties to the extent that your boss reluctantly takes those duties from you. If you had those skills, they would not have to take those duties from you. Sometimes you hear them talk about hiring someone to do something that you could actually do if you just took an extra course.

**Betsy Broke**: What if I'm studying but my interests are not in line with the organisation?

**Silver:** You may be growing but obviously you will not be very useful to the current company. If you want to grow with the company then you should study what would advance the company, and thus render you more valuable, which should lead to your pay increase.

**Robbie Rich:** I never thought I could do things to influence my employer to increase my income. Is there anything else I could do to influence my pay increase?

**Silver:** Improve your performance noticeably. Go the extra mile. If you are in a profit-making organisation, align yourself with the part of the business that brings in more profits. Show that your work is vital in the profitability or productivity of the organisation. Even if you are doing support services, always go the extra mile.

If you are in a non-profit organisation, align yourself with the part of the organisation that brings out the mission and fulfils the objectives better. Make yourself vital in your organisation. Never be seen as extra baggage because if there is downsizing, you might be the first to go.

**Robbie Rich**: Is there another way we can increase our means?

**Silver**: Yes. You can start a part-time business.

**Betsy Broke**: I hate selling. I can't start a selling business.

**Silver**: Frankly, Betsy, everyone is a salesperson. People always talk about things that are interesting to them, often without anyone asking. If you changed your attitude you would find out it's easy. As long as you sell something you already love, you won't even know you are selling. It may be a service or a product. Look within you will find it.

**Robbie Rich**: What about investments?

**Silver:** I suppose you are talking about passive investments? A business is an active investment, because, in addition to you putting your money in, you need to put your energy, skills and talents as well.

Passive investments are also referred to as the "park and pray" method. You give your money to someone else to grow for you and you hope and pray that they know what they are doing.

**Betsy Broke:** Let's not forget we're talking about money to help me to get out of debt. What is the quickest way to make money to help me?

**Silver:** In reality, you should not be looking for quick fixes. The quick fix mentality is what gets a lot of people in "quick debt". Getting out of debt is a process that you need to be patient with. Just like making real lasting extra income. It is also a process that needs to be well thought out for sustainability.

## *Reader Comments*

*Dear Sir, I read your article. It is good, but it being in small print it will escape the attention of a number of people. It is true, one should not borrow simply for consumption. But those are the only loans available in this country at a very high interest. I am seeing lending rate of interest at 30% and above, but no one is willing to give 25% interest rate for savings. Then why and how can people save? Lending institutions, do not care for small savings, as perhaps in this global economy they feel are not cost effective. Lending institutions raise equity capital and issue bonds so that they can have cheaper money, and then lend to the poor people at sky high rates of interest, and still make them the poorest and bonded labourers of lenders for ever. Also plastic money, through credit cards, all encourage loans. Attempt a good article on how to encourage savings also in a small society. What is needed perhaps is aggressive savings plans and not aggressive lending schemes. These are purely my personal thoughts on your article.*

*(Unsigned)*

# 8

## Skills, Talents, And Assets

*"God does not deliver confusion, but he delivers clarity"*

Loral Langemeier

**Robbie Rich:** If I can't get my employer to increase my income regardless of what I do, is there anything else that I could do to increase my income?

**Silver:** There are a lot of things that you could do. We have already alluded to the fact that everyone gets 24 hours per day. We may add here that most people have more skills and talents than they are willing to employ.

**Betsy Broke:** I think the time factor is a real problem. After work, there are house chores and children and homework and all that.

**Robbie Rich:** And to start a business, you need money.

**Silver:** It's not a good idea to focus on the obstacles to your success, otherwise that's all you will ever see before you.

**Betsy Broke:** But it's important to be real.

**Silver:** Your reality was created by you, and it will remain real until you dismantle it and create a new reality.

**Robbie Rich:** So, where do we begin?

**Silver:** You may wish to carry out a full personal audit. Skills audit, talents audit, and assets audit.

**Betsy Broke:** What does that mean?

**Silver:** It means you make a list of all your skills, all your talents, and all your assets.

Betsy Broke: I'm not sure if I can distinguish between skills and talents?

**Silver:** Talents are obviously your natural gifts. These are things that come very easy to you and when you do them, you don't even feel like you are working. Skills are capabilities that you have acquired either by taking a course, an education program, or through practice. You may be a skilled mechanic because you have practiced it a lot under the mentorship of another. Sometimes your skills and your talents are intertwined because the courses or the education you pursued was in line with your talents.

**Robbie Rich:** What is the purpose of doing this personal audit?

**Silver:** You will then identify which skills and talents are employed and are bringing you an income, and which ones are unemployed, and thus not being productive.

**Betsy Broke:** Sounds like that parable of the talents in the Bible where others multiplied their talents and were rewarded, while one hid his talent and was punished.

**Silver:** And if you recall that story, the one who hid his talent was rebuked for laziness, and the talent was taken away from him. The principle with talents is that if you don't use it, you loose it.

**Robbie Rich:** So, I could make extra money if I could identify unemployed skills and talents, and package them and sell them. What is the use of the asset list?

**Silver:** Just like skills and talents, there are some assets that are "lazy assets". They could be making you money but they are not. Some are just taking space and you are never going to use them. You could sell those off, and those that could be employed should be employed.

**Robbie Rich:** So, making extra money is just a question of thinking outside the box. It's so easy to get stuck on the salary when there are so many other possibilities out there. If we could put this into practice, we could work our way out of debt faster by making that extra income and directing it towards the debts. One could also build this extra income for investments. Other than a business, are there any other investing processes that one could follow?

**Silver:** When you D.I.Y[5] your investments, you will require a knowledge base that allows you to calculate the risks and to make decisions. You can D.I.Y a lot of "paper assets", including your stock portfolio on the stock market. You will need

---

[5] D.I.Y = Do It Yourself

to know the how, the what, the when, and the why of buying and selling your shares.

**Betsy Broke**: What are paper assets?

**Silver:** Most financial products are intangible, and are therefore only visible on paper. They have therefore been referred to as paper assets. Real Estate and Traditional businesses that trade stock or merchandise on the other hand, are not paper assets.

### READER COMMENTS

*Hello Nelson, I have been positively motivated by your column, "The Silver Line". I have now made it a habit to always read it whenever I can afford the newspaper. In the newspaper edition of 27th October 2007 you mentioned the essay "The Desire for Prosperity[6]". If it is okay with you please e-mail it to me. I would also like to read any other inspirational/motivational material that you are willing to share with the readers through e-mail. Thanks for the good work. I have managed to get Napoleon Hill's "Think and Grow Rich" from the Internet after reading one of your columns. Thanks again for the great work. MK*

---

[6] This essay can be found in the book: *Your Longing Is Your Calling*, by R.Nelson Letshwene, (Moedi Publishing, 2011) Also available online at www.amazon.com and in digital format on amazon's kindle.

# *9*

# Investing vs. Paying off Debt –
## Rational vs. Psychology

*"Men are anxious to improve their circumstances, but are unwilling to improve themselves; they therefore remain bound."*
James Allen

**Robbie Rich:** There is a debate in my head that I need you to help me to resolve. It is the conflict between paying off debt and investing. Some financial advisors say if the interest on your loan is higher than the interest you are getting on your investments, it is better to focus on paying off debt first, and when you are out of debt, you can focus on investing. But you seem to be saying that I should keep investing even if I'm in debt.
**Silver:** Okay, let's look at both arguments.

**Betsy Broke:** It makes logical sense to focus on paying off debt first to avoid excessive interest.

**Silver:** I am not in disagreement with that proposition. It sounds logical. The only problem with human beings is that they are not always logical. So, let's follow that logic to its end, and then follow the psychology of money that supports my second proposition.

**Robbie Rich:** So, it makes mathematical sense and logic to pay off high interest debt first, and then start investing, right?

**Silver:** First, let's agree that if human beings were rational and logical all the time, they would not be taking these astronomically high interest loans that lands them in trouble. They would not be doing impulse buying that gets their finances in trouble. They would not be in trouble for all the emotional decisions that they have taken. It is curious that when they want to argue for their limitations, they tell you that they're being logical. You can't solve a problem with the same energy that created it.

**Robbie Rich:** It is true that we're not always

logical. But one could argue that there was pressure that led one to make wrong decisions.

**Silver:** And who is to say that pressure will not come again and cause more trouble in your life?

**Betsy Broke:** So, that's why we need to try to apply both logic and psychology to our finances?

**Silver:** We should.

**Robbie Rich:** You've got my attention. How do I follow both logic and psychology in my finances?

**Silver:** Let's follow your logical route to its end first, then we can see where the psychology of money will fit in.

**Robbie Rich:** Okay, my logic says let me pay off the most expensive debt first, and when I've cleared it, I can start investing. The numbers make sense that way.

**Silver:** All things being equal, that might work. Let's follow the numbers. Let's say at your current level of indebtedness, it would take you five years to completely clear your debt. With additional focus from additional income, you could reduce that to three years. The first question you have to answer now is whether you would remain committed and resolute over the next three years to never ever take any additional loans, even if you experience similar pressures that got you to take the current loans that you have.

**Robbie Rich:** If I make a solid commitment, I can stay focused.

**Silver:** So, you commit all your resources to paying off debt, and commit nothing to savings because your argument is that savings interest rates are too low. Let me throw the spanner in the works: the car breaks down, or the geyser leaks, or your child has a school trip, but you have no savings. What do you do?

**Betsy Broke:** That's a tough proposition!

**Silver:** You see, things never remain equal. Something almost always shifts.

**Robbie Rich:** Your psychology is starting to work on me. So, regardless of how much debt I'm in, I should still have savings?

**Betsy Broke:** Otherwise we will take more loans to cover those emergencies!

**Silver:** Let's continue with your logic. One of the things that money needs to grow is time. If you are not saving and investing, what are you losing?

**Robbie Rich:** I lose time. I could reach retirement paying off debt but having no investments. At that point I could be unemployable, debt free, but broke!

**Betsy Broke:** That's a scary thought!

**Silver:** We have arrived at that conclusion by following logic. Now let's look at the psychology of money. Human beings are creatures of habit. You've heard the saying: 'you can't teach an old dog new tricks'. If you are used to the habit of borrowing money for every problem you have, what would get you to give up that habit?

**Robbie Rich:** I thought a new decision and a commitment could?

**Silver:** You need another habit. It takes a new habit to dislodge an old habit. The real reason I prefer that you keep saving money even if you are dealing with debt is that you need to start developing a new habit – the habit of saving.

**Robbie Rich:** Even if the numbers say otherwise?

**Silver:** Yes. It's not the numbers I'm initially concerned with. You need to create new neurological pathways in your brain. The habit of saving will need as much time to be strong, just as the habit of borrowing is strong.

**Robbie Rich:** Besides, I could be encouraged to see my savings going up, even as my debt is going down!

**Silver:** Exactly.

**Betsy Broke:** I didn't get it when you kept mentioning this psychology of money thing. Now I think I see how it works. Last time we had savings we used them to clear debt. And yet we're still in debt!

**Silver:** Many people have been there. They pay off the credit card, or clear the overdraft facility, only to get back into debt again.

**Robbie Rich:** So then we should never use our savings to clear debt!

**Silver:** Have a debt elimination plan and follow it. But you must also have a savings and investment plan and follow it.

**Betsy Broke:** So, now I see why you say we

should allocate a percentage of our income to servicing debt, and also allocate a percentage to the 'pay yourself first' principle.

**Silver:** Yes, sometimes life is not about 'either or', sometimes the answer to life is "both"!

**Robbie Rich:** Now I know, human beings are generally not as logical as they claim to be! People who succeed must have strong success habits!

## READER COMMENTS:

*Hi Nelson! I'm a huge follower of your column and I believe you are really doing a fantastic job of helping [the country] become financially literate. Since 2004 I've had to change the way I think of becoming wealthy and financially literate because of the books you recommended in your column such as Robert Kiyosaki's Rich Dad Poor Dad [series of books]. These days I've amassed a collection of most of the books you recommend like Richard Branson's autobiography, Napoleon Hill's Think and Grow Rich and George Clason's The Richest man In Babylon, and many more. I wonder why we are never taught these things in school! I don't regret a penny I spent because it's my way of investing in my own future and financial intelligence. ... Keep the good work up. Cheers! MK*

# *10*

## Change The Way You Look At Things

*"Change the way you look at things, and the things you look at, will change"*
Dr. Wayne Dyer

**Robbie Rich:** I have heard that life is a matter of perspective. It depends on how you look at things.

**Betsy Broke:** My question would be: is poverty an attitude or a fact? If a person changed their attitude, could they change their circumstances?

**Robbie Rich:** Especially that you could have all the right tools such as higher education and talents, by which you could be rich, but you still continue to struggle to make ends meet.

**Silver:** Those are very good points. While knowledge and education are important, there are other things in life that will help you to have more of what you want and achieve more. Robert Kiyosaki, author of *Rich Dad Poor Dad*, spoke of something he called the BE-DO-HAVE principle.

**Robbie Rich:** What is Be – Do – Have?

**Silver:** Everyone wants the final results. They want to HAVE, but are seldom interested in what comes before that. In this case they have life backwards. That principle means before you can have more, you must BE more, and then do more. So the correct question to ask is: how do I become more, instead of, how do I have more. Unless you learn to be, you will never have more.

**Betsy Broke:** That sounds complicated. Can you explain what you mean?

**Silver:** There is a book by James Allen called *As A Man Thinketh[7], and now* may seem to be a good time to discuss some of the concepts in it.

---

[7] James Allen, As a Man Thinketh, can be downloaded from www.asamanthinketh.net

This book explains that your thoughts make you what you are.

He writes: "*Men are anxious to improve their circumstances, but are unwilling to improve themselves; they therefore remain bound.*"

James Allen gives a few examples. One is of a poor man who is extremely anxious to change his circumstances. However, this man dodges his work, and thinks he is justified to defraud his employer on the grounds of insufficiency of his wages. This man, writes Allen, "does not understand the simplest rudiments of those principles which are the basis of true prosperity, and is not only totally [unfit] to rise out of his [poverty], but is actually attracting to himself a still deeper poverty by dwelling in, and acting out, [lazy], deceptive, and [inhumane] thoughts."

**Betsy Broke:** There is that pervasive attitude that if you perceive your employer to not be paying or treating you right by you, you could do all those negative things.

**Robbie Rich:** I think the principle here is that you cannot succeed by cheating and being half-hearted in what you do.

**Silver:** What goes around comes around. The very same attitude that you think you are directing towards others, works first in yourself.

**Betsy Broke:** You mean if you cheat you will be cheated?

**Silver:** Essentially yes. If you bless, you will be blessed. Allen also gives an example of a rich man who has a disease caused by gluttony. He is willing to give large sums of money to get rid of it, but he will not sacrifice his gluttonous desires. He wants to gratify his taste for rich and unnatural foods and have his health as well. "Such a man", writes Allen, "is totally unfit to have health, because he has not learned the first principles of a healthy life".

**Robbie Rich:** I remember seeing an advert for a pill called "cheat and eat", which said you could eat whatever you want, you then pop the pill in, and it takes care of your troubles.

**Silver:** You can never cheat natural processes. It's like what the late Stephen Covey called 'the law of the farm'. You can't be lazy all summer, and the day before the harvest, throw your seeds in the ground, water and fertilize them and expect a harvest.

**Betsy Broke:** But the story of this rich may also mean that money cannot buy everything.

**Silver:** Mahatma Ghandi said, you need to be what it is you want to see in the world. If you want peace, be peace. You cannot have unless you become.

**Betsy Broke:** I hear those arguments clearly. They seem to advocate the power of the mind that we talked about earlier. The poor man stays in poverty because all he thinks about are thoughts rooted in poverty, and the sick man stays sick because he won't give up the seed of his sickness. But still, how do these connect to your BE-DO-HAVE formula?

**Silver:** Consider the behaviour of the poor man. What is the fuel for such a behaviour?

**Betsy Broke:** I think it comes from his attitude. His entitlement mentality, which actually makes him ungrateful and grumpy.

**Silver:** Exactly. He is being ungrateful. His state

of being is that of ingratitude. From that state of being (BE), come his actions (DO), and from his actions, follows his results, poverty (HAVE). In the book, *Faith and Purpose*[8], this formula is discussed in details.

**Robbie Rich:** And the rich man is Being gluttonous, and thus he continues to eat, and thus get the results of sickness.

**Betsy Broke:** Attitude is everything!

---

[8] R. Nelson Letshwene, 2015, *Faith and Purpose – Living life to the full, without fear, guilt, and regrets*, Moedi Publishing, Also available on amazon.com

*11*

---

# Investing in Residential Real Estate

*"Buying a home is usually a wise financial decision because it allows you to invest your hard-earned income in a real asset that builds equity."*
- Lamar S. Smith

We have a focus on investing in residential real estate.

**Robbie Rich**: What is the best investment one can focus on?

**Silver**: There is no such thing as the best investment for all. It all depends on where you are at in your life. But I am of the strong opinion that even as you are getting out of debt, you should focus on owning your primary home. That would generally be your best investment. Focus on paying it off as quickly as possible.

**Betsy Broke**: Our friends say Real Estate is the best kind of investment. You buy a house and rent it out and it pays for itself. What do you think about that?

**Silver**: There is a big difference between your primary home and your secondary property. Your friends may be talking about a secondary property, which is an investment property. In that case, you always have to keep your eye on the cash flow. If you are having a positive cash flow, and a very low vacancy rate, then you have a good deal. Know that expert real estate investors make money when they buy, and when they sell.

**Robbie Rich**: What do you mean by positive cash flow and a low vacancy rate?

**Silver**: Let me explain positive cash flow by the use of an example. If your mortgage repayment to the bank is say, 3000.00 per month, and your tenant is prepared to pay you say a rental of

3600.00, you have a gross positive cash flow of 600.00 which is 7200 per year. If the cost of maintenance and other running cost per year is say 2200, then you have a positive cash flow of 5 000 per year, which, after taxes, may be okay depending on your goals. If interest rates do not go up, you may be ok for that year.

**Robbie Rich:** Why would a rise in interest rates matter?

**Silver:** A rise in interest rates will increase your repayment to the bank, which will reduce that positive cash flow for the year. If your positive cash flow is too low, a huge jump in interest rates and other costs, or a drop in rentals could wipe out your profits and enter your property in a loss making position and render it not viable.

**Betsy Broke**: But if the markets are flat you must be prepared to accept lower rental, and then top up your mortgage repayment.

**Silver**: Prepared would be the key word Betsy. Being prepared implies that you don't depend on the tenant completely. You have some extra cash that you can put into that mortgage. But the most important question is *why would you be prepared to finance or sponsor someone to stay in your house?* If interest rates go up, you must still be prepared to pop out more. You have to remember the golden rule is that if you are paying more than you are receiving, you are generally not progressing.

**Robbie Rich**: But isn't the house going up in value?

**Silver**: Well yes and no. It may be going up in value, or not, depending on multiple factors including location and the state of the economy. Besides, a valuation report does not put money in your pocket. It only does so the day you sell. If you don't sell and you keep struggling to raise the money to pay the mortgage, then don't call that an investment. Like I said, real estate experts make money when they buy, and when they sell.

If the bank ever forecloses the deal, you lose more than your house, you lose your credit rating as well. And by the way, your credit rating is an asset that you should strive to protect.

**Robbie Rich:** How can you make money when

you buy?

**Silver:** I was hoping you would ask that question. When you buy a property, you have to thoroughly analyse it and make sure that it has positive cash flow from day one. That means, other than the legal costs and perhaps the deposit that your banker asks for, you shouldn't have to continue paying for it over time. Your tenant should "take over" the mortgage payment, including other costs of running the property, and of course provision for your vacancy rate. Your next focus is how quickly can you get your money out.

**Betsy Broke**: You mentioned a vacancy rate, what is that?

**Silver**: That is your estimate of the number of months your house will be without a tenant per year or over the length of the mortgage period. If the rate is say 5%, then over a 20-year period, it means for 12 months you estimate that you won't have a tenant. The deal is only good if during the years that your property is occupied, the income covers this contingency. That way when the house is empty, you won't have to search for money from somewhere else to make the payments. If there is no positive cash flow that would cover this, you might fall behind, and be in danger of losing the house.

**Betsy Broke**: Are you saying we shouldn't get into this kind of investment?

**Silver**: No, all I am saying is: do your homework! There are good deals out there but you must look hard for them, and be prepared! Prepared is the keyword. If the property cannot take care of itself plus put money in your pocket, and I mean real cash, why on earth would you want to buy it and call that an 'investment'?

If investing in residential real estate is your intended mode of creating wealth, I suggest that you read up on the subject. There are a lot of books that shed light on this subject, like *Real Estate Riches*[9], and other books. As you read you will find out that there are other markets within the real estate industry.

---

[9] Dolf de Roos, Ph.D: Real Estate Riches – how to become rich using your banker's money, Warner Business books.

**Robbie Rich:** You mean commercial real estate?

**Silver:** Yes, and many more, but before you go into that, you will find that the residential real estate itself is a huge industry with many different markets. There are houses, apartments, and town houses or what is called condominiums. Each of these have their own separate markets and people who are interested in them. Or, as an investor, you could focus on what the Americans call "fixerupers".

**Betsy Broke:** What are those?

**Silver:** There are investors who buy moderately dilapidated houses, fix them up, and flip them. A fixeruper comes from the words "fix up" or "fix her up". When you buy these, you have to do proper cash flow analysis to ensure that the purchase price, plus the cost of fixing, would still leave room for you to add your profit before your flip them.

**Betsy Broke:** What do you mean flip them?

**Silver:** I'm just preparing you for the terminology you will find in some of these books that you will read. To flip is when you sell the property almost immediately after you fix her up. That means you are not holding it to rent it out. You make your immediate profit because you bought the property at less than the market value, fixed her up at a cost that still allows you to make a profit when you sell it.

**Robbie Rich**: Does the commercial real estate industry also have many different pockets?

**Silver:** Absolutely. You have the office-building sector, which may be slightly more straightforward. Then you get the industrial property market, which comprise mostly of warehouses and industrial space. When you get into the retail sector, you will have to get into details because, as they say, retail is detail.

**Robbie Rich:** What is so different about the retail sector.

**Silver:** Well, one of the distinguishing factors is that your tenants are not treated the same way. You anchor tenant does not get treated the same way as everyone else.

**Betsy Broke:** What's an anchor tenant?

**Silver:** When you think about a shopping mall,

there is always the big supermarket or department store that draws most of the clients to the mall. Then there are other tenants who depend on the traffic that goes to the big grocery or department store. Your anchor tenant will therefore pay less rent per square meter than the smaller tenants. The retail lease can get complicated in that it can include profit sharing and all that.

**Robbie Rich:** So buying a shopping mall is not the same as buying an office building.

**Silver:** Absolutely not. When you get into hotels, you are also in another real estate sector altogether. Here, your 'tenant' may be a one-night guest, and you have other running costs that include a huge support staff. It's a completely different kind of business, albeit real estate based.

**Betsy Broke:** What about buying empty plots of land?

**Silver:** Speculators do that. Empty land does not put money in your pocket, so you must have enough money to carry the cost. Even within this there are different parcels of land packages ranging from undeveloped, semi-developed and developed land.

**Robbie Rich:** Wow, there is more to real estate than I thought. There is much reading to be done.

# *12*

# Are You Preparing to be Prepared?

*"Choices are the building blocks of life"*

**Robbie Rich:** I would really like to revisit that topic of budget allocations. I would like to see how Retirement Planning features on that plan. I also need to understand the rationale behind the other allocations. I need to distinguish between savings of various reasons including the "preparedness" you mentioned as relates to real estate investment planning, and the difference between primary home and investment property.

**Silver:** That's a mouthful. We will take them one by one.

**Robbie Rich:** You said:

- o 10% to saving and investments ("Pay yourself first")

- o   5% to Protection (Insurances)
- o   20% to Debt servicing (if you're in debt, otherwise to investments)
- o   65% to living expenses

**Silver:** I also said this would differ from family to family. The main thing is your reasons and motivations for doing what you're doing. One of the major things that throw people off financially is the amount of money that goes towards consumer debt.

**Robbie Rich:** Perhaps we can start there. First by defining consumer debt and contrasting it with good debt

**Silver:** We have to define both. That which is referred to as good debt should be defined as debt that finances either long lasting assets such as real estate property, or performing assets that generate income.

**Robbie Rich:** That would leave consumer debt to be debt that's financing lifestyle issues?

**Silver:** As long as you remember that lifestyle differs also from person to person or family to family, each according to their means.

**Betsy Broke:** So then some families might be fine financing lifestyle by debt because they can afford it?

**Silver:** It may be a function of disposable cash. Some can "afford" debt, meaning, that nothing else suffers as a result of debt because there is enough cash to go around. Others can't afford debt because as soon as they get into debt, many other areas of their lives are left vulnerable.

**Robbie Rich:** It seems that the best way to deal with this is to get personal financial advice to ensure that you have debt that's equal to you.

**Silver:** That would be the best approach.

**Robbie Rich:** So, let's address savings for "preparedness". What does that mean?

**Silver:** It's your emergencies. You need to define what an emergency would be for you.

**Betsy Broke:** But if you can define it, then it would not longer be an emergency!

**Silver:** Exactly! That is the point! It is the undefined emergencies that land people in big financial troubles.

**Robbie Rich:** What about an emergency such as

death? Is that definable?

**Silver:** If you can define it, you can provide for it. Stating specifically who should get covered in a funeral policy is part of that definition. Taking life insurance cover to ensure that your death does not disrupt your dependents financially is part of the definition.

**Betsy Broke:** What about a car accident that does not kill you but leaves you disabled?

**Silver:** If you can define it like that, you can provide for it. A disability insurance cover would ensure that you would receive an income if you should get disabled.

**Betsy Broke:** What about car break down or unexpected repairs needed on your house?

**Silver:** If you can define it, you can provide for it.

**Robbie Rich:** Aah I see! The emergencies that get us in trouble are the ones we have not bothered to define?

**Silver:** Exactly!

**Betsy Broke:** What if you have defined it, but you have not managed to provide for it yet by the time it happens?

**Silver:** Then you have an emergency on your hands. Your financial problem solving skills must come to the fore.

**Robbie Rich:** So, if I'm not in debt, a lot more of my money could go to my present and my future?

**Silver:** Yes. And if you are in debt, a lot more of your money will go to your past, especially if you are in consumer debt and you are paying for things that you have long consumed or are busy aging even as a lot of your money continues to finance them.

**Betsy Broke:** So then, if I'm prepared to be prepared, then retirement allocations will never fall behind.

**Silver:** Retirement should never be an emergency. It is something we should prepare for throughout our productive time. Sometimes you have to say "no" to the present and to the past, in order to say "yes" to your future, otherwise it will never be financed.

### **Reader Comments:**

*Essence of Budget (I like the topic) That's a fantastic piece of work, Nelson. Lets hope after your crucial advise to do personal budgeting all citizens will make a change in their lives. Yes there's always a Silver Line, all you need is to look for it; I don't want to be like Betsy Broke, Rose T.*

# *13*

---

# Earned or Passive income?

*"Don't borrow from your financial future, but plan so that, with the aid of your investments with capital growth, you can borrow from your financial past."*
Nico Swart.

Let's talk about financial independence and financial planning.

**Robbie Rich**: What is financial independence and how do I get there?
**Silver Line**: Well, financial independence means different things to different people. For most people it means not depending on the state but on your own resources that you saved up before your retire. That may include your own pension or

other sources of income.

**Betsy Broke:** Does it mean you are wealthy?

**Silver**: Not necessarily. It may just mean you are not begging from anyone. You are financially independent.

**Robbie Rich**: How does one plan to be financially independent?

**Silver**: Well, first you must invest in your own education about how money works. You will not just wake up one day and find yourself financially independent, just because you have worked for 40 years.

**Betsy Broke:** Doesn't everyone know how money works? What are the different aspects of financial education?

**Silver**: If everyone knew how money works then we wouldn't be having as many bankruptcies and insolvencies as we are having, would we? Financial literacy is the key to personal financial education. Can you speak the language of money? Do you have its vocabulary? You must understand the different kinds of incomes and decide how to accumulate your money.

**Robbie Rich:** Aren't all incomes the same?

**Silver:** No, there are generally two kinds of incomes: Earned income and passive income. I'd like to add a third category, which I call business income; some may classify this under passive income. Earned income is where almost everyone starts. It is directly related to the amount of work you do. You work you get it, if you don't work, you don't get it.

**Robbie Rich:** Are you implying that passive income is a progression from earned income?

**Silver:** Yes, and no. Once you have earned your money, if you learn how money works, then you can employ it to work for you to produce passive income, or business income. If you never learn how money works, then you could be stuck here for the rest of your life, working for money.

**Robbie Rich:** What is the difference between passive income and business income?

**Silver:** Passive income can be earned through avenues like real estate and royalties. Business income, however, comes from the effective operation of your business. Learning skills to leverage and optimise your resources to a point where they produce residual income for you, for the rest of your life. A few people earn their money this way. The majority depend on earned income. If you take your financial education seriously, however, you will learn investment strategies and business strategies that can catapult you into greatness, financially speaking.

**Betsy Broke:** Are you saying the best investment I can make right now is to invest in my financial education?

**Silver:** Financial ignorance is the cause of poverty, not lack of resources. As Robert Kiyosaki says, there are only two things you can invest: time and money. If you don't have money, you better invest time. Those who invest the time almost always get the money.

**Betsy Broke:** Are there some books you can recommend where I can get started.

**Silver:** There are plenty of books that would address different areas of personal financial management and investments, depending what your current focus is on. If you want to follow some of the concepts we have discussed here in details, you could start with *The Money Field*, and *Seven Essential Money Skills*; and then I suggest that you get into the "Dummy" series of books or the "Idiot Guides" covering new topics in which you would like to get ahead.

**Betsy Broke:** Oh no! You don't expect me to get into a bookstore to purchase an Idiot's Guide to personal finance or Personal Finance for Dummies do you?

**Silver:** I do. Only the wise would dare do that. These books are great for beginners. If you were studying MBA, wouldn't you go and buy MBA for Dummies to learn about different research methodologies that you would otherwise struggle with?

## *Reader Comments:*

*Dumela Rre Letshwene (Greetings Mr Letshwene); I've been following your column for some time. It's quite a very important and beneficial subject that you are dealing with...'Success Or Rather Achieving Success'. Why I am writing this note is to acknowledge the scope and breadth of your reading...Brian Tracy....I subscribe to his newsletters but haven't bought any of his books yet. I am currently reading the Law Of Success course by Napoleon Hill. Having appreciated the vacuum that exist in our education system...lack of goal development or direction...I wish you could consider particularly directing your writings to students at all level....that would be service at its best for this nation...you are doing good man...Thanks. Marshall.*

# *14*

---

# Man is a Creature of Habit

*"Until you make the unconscious conscious, it will
direct your life and you will call it fate."*

Carl Jung

**Silver:** Napoleon Hill writes: "Millions of people
go through life in poverty and want, because they
have made destructive use of the Law of Habit.
Not understanding either the Law of Habit or the
Law of Attraction through which 'like attracts like',
those who remain in poverty seldom realise that
they are where they are as the result of their own
acts."

**Betsy Broke:** Their own acts? Isn't that a harsh
thing to say? Surely you can't blame me for the
circumstances that I find myself in?

**Silver:** Sure. There will always be circumstances. In all circumstances you have a choice. You can join in and be part of those circumstances, and thus have the outcomes of your life be determined for you, or you can manufacture your own. Do you believe in the Law of Compensation?

**Robbie Rich:** What is the law of Compensation?

**Silver:** That Law says you reap what you sow. Ralph Waldo Emerson wrote in 1841: "*Every act rewards itself… Crime and punishment grow out of the same stem …Cause and effect, means and ends, seed and fruit, cannot be severed; for the effect already blooms in the cause, the end pre-exists in the means, the fruit in the seed.*"

**Robbie Rich:** That sounds like a complicated way of saying I need to watch everything I do.

**Betsy Broke:** I don't see how these dead authors you keep quoting could understand how the world has changed since they last wrote those words. Some people are born into poverty through no doings of their own. Besides, how does all that help me to make more money?

**Silver:** Good questions and observations. Havn't you heard of rags to riches stories? Some people, born in poverty, overcome it and become wealthy, and others settle. Money is a fruit. The question is: What is the seed? Where is the tree, or what is the tree? Being born into poverty is not a death sentence. If you looked deep within, you will find that everyone is born with a seed. That seed needs to be planted.

**Robbie Rich:** My chosen vocation should be the tree, I think.

**Betsy Broke:** In that case, I feel like I planted a thorn-bush! I get nothing but trouble from my work.

**Silver:** Would you really say it's from your work?

**Betsy:** Is that not what we are saying?

**Silver:** Two people could be doing the same work, but they will have different experiences because of what they put into their jobs.

**Betsy:** You mean attitude?

**Silver:** That too, but mostly it's habbit.

**Betsy:** What would be the difference?

**Silver:** Habbit is a protracted or continous way of

being. You can temporarily change your attitude, but habbit is something you will always go back to, if you don't uproot the undesirable ones.

**Robbie Rich:** So if I cultivated my vocation through extra studying and learned new method of doing my job, and got into the right habits, I could reap more fruit from it?

**Silver:** That is correct. There are success habits, and there are failure habbits. Don't forget to cultivate the habit of saving as well. If you make more money but you continue with the habit of spending and getting into more debt, you will not make progress. Let me share with you a story by one of the readers of my weekly column in the Botswana Guardian, *Silverline,* who decided to change his mind.

### Reader Comments

> *"I am not so into newspaper reading but I kind of stumbled into your "Silver Line" column and actually read it. Only then did I realise what a dumb and ignorant person I have been - "money wise". With money I have*

*never been calm, never! When I have money all I think about is [The Shopping Malls] .... get my picture? ... Now after reading your column I can actually get calm with the knowledge that it's my money and no one will take it from me unless I give it away. So I am learning to budget, I've been working five years and I have never budgeted before. I've always done impulse buying. All the three cars I've been through were all on impulse. So I am really learning to be calm about money. Ahhh, it's a great feeling really! Knowing you got money in the bank, makes me look good too. Yeah money comes in and finds money... Sweet.''*

**Robbie Rich:** So anyone can change, if they set their mind to it. The devil is in the mind.

**Silver:** So is the Angel; especially the Angel. Putting a little thought into every act that you do will go a long way in determining that you live your life on purpose. As Ralph Waldo Emerson said, circumstances don't make a man, they define him.

**Betsy Broke:** So, the bottom line is that I need to be aware of my habits. And be aware of what results I have been getting from my behaviours. I need to find what seeds I have within me, and what I can do to plant my seeds, and keep observing what fruit is manifesting in my life.

**Silver:** You cannot change what you can't identify.

# 15

## Your Money's Friends and Foes

*"The saving of money is solely a matter of habit"*
Napoleon Hill.

**Betsy Broke:** Many people have savings accounts and they try to save every month, but still they don't get anywhere in terms of accumulating money. What is the cause of that?

**Silver:** Any account that is accompanied by an Automated Teller Machine (ATM) Card should hardly be called a savings account. It's more like a spending account. Especially that most of these ATM cards are also debit cards, which can be used to make purchases in stores and online. Unless you have great discipline, money saved in such a transactional account is set up to be spent.

**Robbie Rich:** Does saving money really work?

**Silver:** You ask like someone who's never experimented with the process.

**Robbie Rich:** Or tried and failed?

**Silver:** Consider this: While there are many studies out there for various reasons, some have estimated that only 6 out of every 100 people aged 25 today will be financially independent in 40 years time. (That is when they are 65 years old). They estimate also that 34 people will have passed away (depending on the country and mortality rates). 10 will be drawing a government pension (more in different countries, especially third world countries), 20 will still be working and 30 will be dependent on relatives.

**Robbie Rich:** I'm not sure if we really trust these statistics?

**Silver:** That is also true. But I think most statistics are obviously based on certain samples and one may always say that they are there to drive a certain agenda.

**Robbie Rich:** I guess you should only consider them to the extent that they apply to you?

Silver: They may serve as a wake up call. Another one from Old Mutual Corporate Retirement Monitor (2017) says "94% of South Africans cannot afford to maintain their standard of living once they retire. Those who contribute to a pension fund for 40 years can still see an income drop of 20% at retirement.[10]"

**Betsy Broke:** But aren't we having more educated people today that are working hard, and therefore should do better?

**Silver:** Well, that is the irony of it. Most people don't actually realise that despite their strong work ethic, hard work alone will not help them in accumulating wealth and becoming financially independent. And being educated in your particular field does not necessarily mean that you understand financial matters.

**Robbie Rich:** So you have to work smarter not just harder, as the saying goes?

---

[10] Milpark Education, 2019, Case Study PGCSTU-8 19a, Cape Town

**Silver:** Working 'smart' is an overrated statement whose meaning eludes many people because they can't translate it to real practicality.

Hear this: It is said that as a teenager, John D. Rockefeller, who later became one of the richest men in America earned $1 hoeing potatoes for a neighbour. He later collected $3.50 interest on a loan he had made to another farmer a year earlier. He learned very early that his hard labour was not enough, and he tapped into the world of compound interest.

**Inflation ...**

**Robbie Rich:** But isn't inflation competing with the interest that you are likely to earn on your saved money?

**Silver:** Well, inflation is a real enemy to your money and you will do well to understand it.

**Betsy Broke:** How does inflation erode my money?

**Silver:** It erodes the purchasing power of money,

so that a thousand bucks of today may be worth less in the future. For example, it is estimated that the US Dollar has lost 90% of its buying power since 1950.

**Commodities ...**

**Robbie Rich:** That means it is not necessarily commodities like gold that are getting more expensive, but it is the dollar losing its value as well?

**Silver**: That is the most likely truth. Gold is a special subject that we should discuss at some point. The high price does not mean that gold has not increased in value over time on its own account.

**Betsy Broke:** Are you saying the general increase in prices is really due to falling currencies instead of increasing value of commodities?

**Silver:** Well, gold is still gold and oil is till oil isn't it? Of course the thing that affects their price is often their scarcity. When markets perceive that there is not enough oil, then the competition raises the price. But there is still a good argument to say that some of that price increase is due to the decreasing value of the currency, or even oil cartels manipulating prices.

**Corporations ...**

**Robbie Rich:** How does one face this battle?

**Silver:** The trouble is we base wealth on currencies.

**Betsy Broke:** Isn't having more money the sign of real wealth?

**Silver:** Well, yes and no. If you study the lives of the richest people in the world today, you will actually find that they don't hold their wealth in their own names, but rather they use corporations. They hold nothing in their names but they control everything. They control corporations, and they own businesses and lots of income producing assets.

**Betsy Broke:** So it's better to own income producing assets like businesses than real cash?

**Silver:** Liquidity is a very important part of your portfolio. Having emergency cash or near cash instruments is very important. But it is true that real wealth cannot be held in cash.

**Betsy Broke:** So the idea that we need to save money, also means we should be aware of enemies such as inflation and the falling values of currencies?

**Silver:** Investing is both art and science.

# *16*

# F I R E

## Financially Independent and Retire Early

### Saving and Investing for FIRE!

F I R E is an acronym of *Financially Independent and Retire Early*. First we will have to define what being financially independent is, and then define what early retirement is or means.

In a nutshell, financial independence is a principle that implies that you depend on your own available resources for your livelihood. There is financial independence for investment purposes as defined by the Securities Exchange Commission that sets levels of passive income from investments. Then there is financial independence defined by various other parties that have interest in your affairs. Tax authorities sets levels at which they feel they can take a lot more from you than from others.

Warren Buffett differentiates between the rich and the wealthy using only one yardstick: mode of travel. He says while the wealthy and the rich are the same in a lot of respects, the wealthy will differentiate themselves from the rich by the way they travel. While the rich may travel business class or first class, the wealthy use private jets. Other than that, they may even live in the same street, eat the same food, and socialise with the same group.

President Barack Obama said there's only so much you can eat in a day, or so much of everyday needs you can fulfil. The rest of the money, you can share with others.

There are many other ways people define their own financial independence. Others talk about downgrading from a high cost lifestyle to an average or low cost lifestyle. Others move from expensive cities to affordable towns. Others redefine what is essential and what's not, or that which is often referred to as needs vs. wants.

Others use numbers such as the 4% rule, which says if they withdrew and lived on only 4% per year of their Retirement Savings, they can live without exhausting their funds in perpetuity. One might argue that that depends on the growth levels of those funds, as well as inflation, which themselves are economic variables.

So now, decide what your level of financial independence entails. The basics are that you must have enough passive income to live the kind of lifestyle you choose or define. Passive income, by definition, does not include active economic activity for the generation of that income, hence, retirement.

Now to the definition of early retirement: Early retirement is the earliest time at which you can achieve your financial independence as you have defined it.

That may not say much because more often than not, retirement date is defined by your pension fund, and early retirement may be a time prior to a time defined by your pension fund. The problem with retiring before your pension fund says you can retire is that, that is referred to as a withdrawal and not a retirement, and that leads to withdrawal taxes. Now when the tax authorities penalise you for your "early retirement" through taxes, that may defeat your 'early retirement' because taxes will reduce the amount that would be generating your passive income.

So then, early retirement can be a function of time or of resources. Early can mean 'before a particular age', or as soon as you reach a certain amount of money or income producing assets or investments.

## WHY?

Why indeed! The motivation for early retirement is key. It would not be enough to just say you want to retire because you are tired of working. It would also not be enough to say because you want to rest.

Indeed, it has been said that some people's work is so much part of their lives that if they stop, they die early. Regardless of its apparent frustrations, perhaps you thrive in the solving of such life's problems.

Some people have found that taking a one-year sabbatical gives them enough rest to allow them to repurpose their lives and get back, maybe not in the thick of things, but perhaps in the thick of thin things.

Retirement may also mean retiring from one profession in order to engage another profession.

Others retire in order to pursue more personal passions. They may want to give more time to the pursuit of the spiritual journey – reading more, contemplating more, praying more, meditating more. Other personal passions may be engagement with the arts – painting, writing, music, charity, or more family time.

As you can see, there is no such thing as retiring to do nothing. Some passions or pursuits may cost you more than others.

### *READER COMMENTS*

*Dumelang (Greetings), I always make sure that I read your articles in the Botswana Guardian, you are doing a very good job of informing us about the financial matters and please keep doing so. I have very little knowledge about "shares" on the Stock Exchange. I would like to know if an ordinary man like me can buy shares on the stock exchange and how to go about it. Please also advice if it is a good idea to invest in shares rather than just saving the money in the bank or buying insurance policies. NL.*

# 17

---

# Do You Believe in Yourself?

*"There's what happened to you in your life, and then there's what you decided it meant. Change your conclusions ... and you can change the way you live your life today."*
Evans – author of Travelling Free

In "*The Power of Positive Thinking*", Norman Vincent Peale says that unless you have a positive attitude about yourself and your abilities, "you cannot be successful or happy."

Yes, you need a positive attitude to be happy. But, as Michael Masterson, author of *Automatic Wealth* says, you can be quite successful by most conventional measurements simply by applying some of the following strategies as well:

Decide exactly what it is you want, make it a primary goal, establish a series of yearly, monthly, weekly, and daily objectives to achieve that goal, Resist the urge to give up along the way. And there will be many urges to give up.

Experience proves that by doing this consistently, you can achieve almost anything you want in life - even if you don't have much faith in your own abilities. You see, it is the doing that builds your faith in yourself. If you do nothing, you strengthen your weaknesses. If you do something, you put doubt to your doubts, and build faith in your faith.

But what if you want happiness? Or, what if, in fact, happiness and calmness are integral to your definition of success? Well, then you need to follow Peale's advice and start thinking positive thoughts about yourself. Let's look at some of the points that Peale makes in his book, *The Power of Positive Thinking*.

Lack of self-confidence, Peale said, "is one of the great problems besetting people today." He makes reference to a survey of college students indicating that for 75% of them, confidence was the thing most lacking in their life.

If you've ever choked up in an interview, forgotten your lines in a play, or been verbally stifled by a rude comment, you know too well the effect that a lack of self-confidence has on performance. The things that nibble at our self-confidence may be in plain sight or take us by surprise.

"The blows of life, the accumulation of difficulties, the multiplication of problems tend to sap energy and leave you spent and discouraged," Peale says. "In such situations", he continues, "it is easy to lose track of your abilities and powers".

But, by re-appraising your personal assets, taking a fresh look at your abilities objectively, you can convince yourself that "you are less defeated than you think you are."

As an example, Peale tells how he counselled a 52-year-old man who came to him "in great despondency." Everything in his life, the man said, had been "swept away" by a recent business setback. "Everything I built up over a lifetime is gone."

Peale recognized that although the man had indeed experienced a serious setback, his chief problem was the way he viewed it. "Suppose we take a piece of paper and write down the values you have left," he suggested. And so they did. Among other things, the list included these personal assets: a wonderful wife - and a 30-year marriage; three devoted children; admiring friends happy to help; good physical health; integrity, and other great qualities, seemingly invisible to the eye.

That's not a bad list. And, if you're feeling down, I would hope that focusing on positive personal assets like these could help you overcome the worst feelings you could possibly have about yourself.

If your previous confidence was based on the external things and the perceptions of other people, you might need to look within to re-evaluate the very qualities that helped you to achieve those external things. In the beginning, when you did not have all that you lost, you had other strengths that pushed you to achieve those things. At what point did your confidence move from yourself to the external things?

Self-confidence is confidence in the Real Self, not just the accumulations you have.

# *18*

## When Budgets Fail, Then What?

*"I get the facts, I study them rationally, I apply imagination."*

Bernard Baruch

**Betsy Broke:** There are times when all budgets just fail, it does not matter what you do. There just is no money. How do you proceed from there?

**Silver:** Money for what?

**Betsy Broke:** Money for life ... there is no money ... what do I do? Do I now go to moneylenders?

**Silver:** The question remains: money for what? You can't get so vague. You have to identify the exact place where you urgently need the money.

**Betsy Broke:** No food, no transport money, the electricity is cut off. It is a crisis.

**Silver:** How much money remains in your pride account?

**Betsy Broke:** Pride account? I have no such account. I have no money!

**Silver:** It would be best to calm down first. Then think. You pride account is for Ego-boosters. Can you try humble pie? If you have generally been disciplined and just this one time things went out of control, it surely is easy to get back on track. You always want to identify where things went out of hand so that you don't repeat the experience next month.

**Betsy Broke:** Well, if I just had to have that winter jacket or there was no way I could avoid that expense. I mean this occasion comes only once a year.

**Silver:** Well, now that you have identified the extraordinary expense, and you know it comes once a year, now you know that next year you would have to include in the budget. Now what can you cut on next month to make sure that things don't get out of hand for a long time?

**Betsy Broke:** I can deal with that next month, but right now I need some cash.

**Silver:** Well, if you can decide now that next month you are prepared to go without some particular item or expense such as your cable TV subscription, then you can borrow the equivalent of that amount now. But if you don't identify the item in next month's budget that should cover the hole that you created now, guess what, this problem will not go away.

**Betsy Broke:** Cable TV? What about my favourite programs?

**Silver:** It is time to weigh your priorities now and take a deliberate decision. Perhaps it's your food budget, or your going out money, but something has to give, if you want to stay in control.

**Betsy Broke:** So jumping to borrow money without knowing exactly how I am going to repay it is what gets me in trouble in the first place?

**Silver:** Exactly, that is how most people get in trouble. Giving a little thought to everything that you do keeps you away from going with the flow, and keeps you in control.

**Betsy Broke:** What if what I am prepared to go without next month does not give me enough money to cover what I need now?

**Silver:** Then you keep looking in that budget. Perhaps you can go without that particular thing for two months. The key is to stay calm, and give a thought to everything that you do. Otherwise find a way to make extra money, which is actually a lot easier than trying to limit yourself.

**Betsy Broke:** If that were easier don't you think I could have gone there first? How can making extra money be easier?

**Silver:** Well, think outside the box. Is there some item in your house that is actually still valuable, that however, is currently of no use to you? Can you sell that and stay afloat financially?

**Betsy Broke:** Well, I may not be using some items but they actually have sentimental value, and I can't just get rid of them because I need cash.

**Silver:** That's a fair point. But what sentimental

value do the clothes that don't fit you any more hold? Could you just be holding on to the past? You know if you could empty that wardrobe or that garage or that room that has been turned into a store room, you could be inspired to buy new things instead of holding on to the past. You might actually feel better about un-cluttering your life.

**Betsy Broke:** I need to find a way to avoid such cash emergencies, they drive me nuts.

**Silver:** The sooner you start putting money into that emergency account, the sooner you can take care of such emergencies without fretting.

**Betsy Broke:** Let's go back to that "pride account". How do I identify it?

**Silver:** Sometimes there are things that are so much part or our lives that living without them would seem catastrophic. They may just be habits that cost you money, and if you changed them, you could actually save money.

**Betsy Broke:** So I should start looking at my habits, and figuring out which part of my ego they're feeding, and at what cost?

**Silver:** That's one way. Another way is to look at the whole structure of your finances and see what's going on. Some things would be more sensitive than others. For example, your children have always gone to this particular school, which costs you so much, and yet there are perfectly comparable schools that cost less, would you consider that part of your structure?

**Betsy Broke:** That would be difficult.

**Silver:** Or maybe consider your entire lifestyle. What is it costing you? What would happen if you drastically changed?

**Betsy Broke:** Drastically?

**Silver:** Drastically. Do you need two cars? Or do you need a car at all? Is there a safe way to travel like a reliable public transport where you live? What do your hobbies cost you? Could you change your hobbies? Sometimes they don't take money from you, but they take valuable time that could be used to create an extra income.

**Betsy Broke:** That sounds drastic.

**Silver:** Or consider where you live. Do you need to be living there? Could you pay less for rent if you went elsewhere? Or, if it's your own home you live in, if you rented it out to someone else and you went a paid less rent elsewhere, would that work?

**Betsy Broke:** That's thinking way outside the box! Maybe I need a new job in a new town.

**Silver:** Sometimes that's what it may take. Sometime people are even afraid to get a new job in the same town because it would rattle their cage, let alone a new town.

# *19*

## Don't Criticize Yourself!

*"The only thing that you ever have any control of is your current thinking."*
Louise Hay

**Silver:** James Allen's book, *As a Man Thinketh*, emphasises the power of thought to influence our lives. The thoughts we think and the feelings we experience create who we become.

**Robbie Rich:** I think the one thing that holds most of us back is self-criticism which leads to low self-esteem.

**Silver:** Unfortunately criticism never changes anything other than make you feel less than you are and hold you back. You need to refuse to criticize yourself. When you criticize yourself, you are giving yourself a negative direction. When you approve of yourself, your changes are positive.

**Betsy Broke:** I think the one question in most of our minds that stop us from making progress in any direction is: What if I make mistakes?

**Robbie Rich:** The problem with that question is that it often produces fear, caution, and a judgemental attitude of, I told you so!

**Betsy Broke:** How do you deal with such issues?

**Silver:** First, you need to stop scaring yourself so much. Stop terrorizing yourself with your thoughts. Your fears are only thoughts they are not real. You can replace those thoughts with empowering beautiful thoughts that will propel you forward. And if you make mistakes, which you invariably will, you need to learn to forgive yourself. Let the past go. You did your best with the knowledge and understanding you had at the time. You did not go out of your way to destroy your life or anybody else's for that matter. Holding thoughts of forgiveness for yourself and for others strengthens you.

**Robbie Rich:** I think you need to praise yourself for every baby step you take.

**Silver:** Anthony Robbins, author of *Awaken the Giant Within*, captured it when he said most people rebuke themselves when they mess up but they don't reward themselves when they do the right things. He said, for example, if you are trying to lose weight, don't wait until you have lost a pound to reward yourself, but the moment you push away the plate with the food still on it, that is a victory. Criticism breaks down the inner spirit. Praise builds it up. Carry positive affirmations in your pocket and repeat them to yourself throughout the day.

**Betsy Broke:** What kind of affirmations? I mean, we are always affirming one thing or another.

**Silver:** Positive statements that you repeat to yourself everyday to remind yourself to be positive. In her book, *I Can Do It*, Louise Hay[11] explains that every word you speak is an affirmation. You are affirming and creating your

---

[11]Louise Hay, *I Can Do It: How To Use Affirmations To Change Your Life,* Hay house.

life experience with every word and thought. She discusses health, forgiveness, prosperity, creativity, relationships, job success, and self-esteem.

**Robbie Rich**: So I can create positive affirmations for every area of my life?

**Silver:** An affirmation like – "I have unlimited choices. Opportunities are everywhere" – helps you to start looking out for opportunities instead of entertaining the complaints of others.

**Robbie Rich:** Another affirmation from Hay's book is: "I move from poverty thinking to prosperity thinking, and my finances reflect this change".

**Betsy Broke:** I think I'm going to like this. How about this one: "I radiate success and prosper wherever I turn."

**Silver:** Those are some powerful affirmations that you can use every morning.

**Betsy Broke:** But, am I not lying to myself when I'm saying a thing that I know not to be currently true?

**Robbie Rich:** But many of the negative ones we

repeat may also not be true until they become true.

**Silver:** The use of affirmations could be tricky for people who are not used to them. It is easier for many people to argue for their limitations than to argue for their prosperity.

**Betsy Broke:** What do you mean I'm arguing for my limitations?

**Silver:** By defending negativity in your life, you are arguing for your limitations.

**Betsy Broke:** But one could say that I'm talking about reality.

**Silver:** It became real because you gave it so much energy. Life is not just about strategies. It is about our belief systems as well. You become what you think about.

To create a positive life, you will need to eliminate the voice of doubt and hear the true word from within. In the book, *Faith and Purpose*[12], this subject is covered more extensively. You will do

---

[12] R. Nelson Letshwene, 2015, Faith and Purpose – Living Your Life to the full without Fear, Guilt or regrets; Moedi publishing; also available from amazon.com

well to read it. By using affirmations, you are creating your future. You repeat these words daily until you believe them and act on them.

So In summary, Don't criticize yourself, don't scare yourself, forgive yourself, praise yourself, and practice daily affirmations.

## *Reader comments*

*Hi, I am not a frequent reader of columns in the newspapers, but today I just decided to read your column because it focused on mistakes that we make as human beings. Coincidentally, two days back somebody reminded me of my bad mistakes committed around 1999 - 2003 and I told that person that I am not interested in the past because my mistakes have brought out something positive in me!! I am now a very caring and compassionate person compared to the person I was during the cited time.*

*I want to thank you so much for the revelation you made in your column because some people are so into the past they cannot move on with life and enjoy it. In the process such people make life for other people very difficult!! I am only praying to God that they read your column for this week.*

*If possible, please publish something on "Men and Forgiving/ Forgetting" and also "Men and Their Mothers - how this can destroy relationships with spouses/ girlfriends." I believe a lot of relationships are suffering because of these two issues and you can make a breakthrough for some agonized individuals like me.*

*Thank You, L. (If by any chance you publish this letter, please do not write my surname).*

\*\*

# *20*

---

# Questions to Consider before your Invest

*"If you don't know yourself, the market is an expensive place to find out."*
Adam Smith

**Betsy Broke:** I have asked before about investing in shares and you still have not answered me.

**Silver:** Well, I will answer you by asking you four questions. If you answer NO to all four questions, I suggest you shelf the issue of shares until a later discussion.

**Robbie Rich:** What are the four questions?

**Silver:** The questions are:

1. Right now, can you comfortably cover your living expenses, including food and shelter without borrowing for any of these?

2. Do you have enough cash for emergencies?

3. Do you have adequate insurance to protect your family?

4. Are you saving adequately for retirement regularly?

**Robbie Rich:** Why are these questions important?

**Silver:** Well, if you answered them in the affirmative, then you might have some money to put towards risky investments. If your answer is NO, then honestly, you don't have a strong enough foundation financially to venture out into the unknown world.

Robbie Rich: They all require some measurements. What if I can answer yes to all questions, but add that I'm not sure what enough is?

Silver: These questions are important to consider

fully, and to come up with your own levels of what's enough. You may need to consult with a financial planner who will help you to determine the right levels for you and your family.

**Robbie Rich:** Are you saying I should not invest on the stock market at all until I have fully answered these questions?

**Silver:** Not necessarily. But there is no point going to complex investment scenarios when you have not answered the basic ones. These questions speak to your foundation.

**Betsy Broke:** Are there any other questions I should consider?

**Silver:** The following questions will help you to know yourself in three areas: Your time horizon, your risk tolerance level, and your investment objectives.

**Robbie Rich:** Let's talk about time horizon, what is that?

**Silver:** Consider these questions: first, how long can you afford to leave your nest egg untouched so that it can grow? Less than five years or more than ten years?

**Betsy Broke:** For me it's more like less than 60 days, if that!

**Silver:** It's great to be honest and to know exactly where you are. At this stage, that means you don't even have a nest egg, you are still grappling with issues of laying a foundation. Once the foundation is laid, the further you are from retirement, the more time you have to allow your money to grow. Compound interest spoken of by George Clason in *The Richest Man in Babylon* requires time.

The next question is: What will your cash needs be in the next five years?

**Betsy Broke:** It sounds like this financial freedom will take longer than I thought.

**Robbie Rich:** Well, school fees, mortgage repayments, and car repayment will occupy our budget for some time to come. Not to mention getting out of debt and refurnishing our house ...

**Silver:** Just remember: include yourself among those you love. School fees for your children are important but don't ignore your own education. Besides, if you stay positive, the universe will assist you in your endeavours, then that freedom will not be that far off.

If you are older or have a medical condition, then medical costs are the issues to plan for. The next question in the time horizon sphere is: how dependent are you on your present income?

**Betsy Broke:** It seems I'm failing because I depend entirely on my income and it is not even enough.

**Silver:** In life, there are no right or wrong answers like in school. This is just an opportunity to know yourself. The first three questions help you to figure out whether your foundations are laid and you are ready to take risk, while the rest of the questions help you to plan with time in mind. Too many people waste one of the most valuable resources they have.

**Robbie Rich:** Which one is that?

**Silver:** TIME. Next, we will focus on Risk tolerance and investment objectives.

---

# 21

---

# The Value of Time[13]

*"Practice Random Kindness and senseless acts of
beauty. It is positive anarchy, disorder, a sweet
disturbance!"*

Adair Lara

(From Chicken Soup for the Soul 2)

Imagine there is a bank which credits your
account each morning with $86,400, carries over
no balance from day to day, allows you to keep
no cash balance, and every evening cancels
whatever part of the amount you had failed to use
during the day.

What would you do? Draw out every cent, of

---

[13] https://marliescohen.com/the-value-of-time/

course!

Well, everyone has such a bank.

It's name is TIME.

Every morning, it credits you with 86,400 seconds. Every night it writes off, as lost, whatever of this you have failed to invest to good purpose. It carries over no balance. It allows no overdraft.

Each day it opens a new account for you. Each night it burns the records of the day. If you fail to use the day's deposits, the loss is yours. There is no going back. There is no drawing against the "tomorrow". You must live in the present on today's deposits. Invest it so as to get from it the utmost in health, happiness and success!

The clock is running. Make the most of today...

To realize the value of ONE YEAR...

Ask a student who has failed his final exam.

To realize the value of ONE MONTH...

Ask a mother who has given birth to a pre-mature

baby.

To realize the value of ONE WEEK...

Ask an editor of a weekly newspaper.

To realize the value of ONE DAY...

Ask a daily wage labourer who has ten kids to feed.

To realize the value of ONE HOUR...

Ask the lovers who are waiting to meet.

To realize the value of ONE MINUTE...

Ask the person who has just missed the train.

To realize the value of ONE SECOND...

Ask a person who has survived an accident.

To realize the value of ONE MILLI-SECOND...

Ask a person who has won a silver medal in the Olympics.

Treasure every moment that you have! And treasure it more because you shared it with someone special...

special enough to have some of your time!!!

So tell me... what are you going to do with your 86,400 seconds TODAY?

# 22

# How Much Can You Afford to Lose?

*"Thinking is the hardest and most exhausting of all labour; and hence many people shrink from it. We never move forward until we begin to think."*
Wallace D. Wattles

**Betsy Broke:** What is risk tolerance?

**Silver:** Risk is the measure of your willingness and ability to see your investments shrink. So we have to speak of risk tolerance and risk capacity. So another way to ask this question is: How much can you afford to lose?

**Robbie Rich:** Now isn't it true that the higher the risk, the higher the return?

**Silver:** Before we get to that idea, we have to look at these two concepts objectively. Your risk capacity can be measured quantitatively, whereas your risk tolerance may be a factor of your emotional engagement with risk.

**Robby Rich:** How do you measure risk capacity?

**Silver:** It starts with looking at your foundation and your protection. If your foundation is right, and your protection is adequately in place, we can estimate that if you invested a certain amount, and you lost it all, the loss would not affect you adversely.

**Robbie Rich:** Meaning that I can stomach the loss?

**Silver:** Meaning you financial life won't fall apart because of that loss.

**Robbie Rich:** So does high risk always equal high return?

**Silver:** High risk does not always equal a return. If there was such a guarantee then we would not be speaking of risk. But when you do get a return, it may usually be higher and compensates for the risk you took. But the challenge is your willingness to face the risk.

**Betsy Broke:** If the return is high, then shouldn't everyone take risk?

**Silver:** The return is not guaranteed. Neither is the loss. Either one can happen. You can lose it all. That is what you must be prepared to face first and foremost. That speaks of your risk tolerance. If you are prepared to lose, then when you win, it's a bonus.

Billionaire J. Paul Getty was well known for hitting dry holes in his oil investments. But he did believe in finding oil. So he was prepared to invest as much money as it took to get oil. While he lost a lot, when he did get an oil well, the rewards were tremendous. That is why the correct question to deal with risk tolerance is always: how much can you afford to lose?

**Robbie Rich:** So, affordability is the determining factor. That seems to relegate investing to having excess cash.

**Silver:** That is why the three questions we asked previously are so important. They cover insurance, emergency fund, and current living expenses. These, you cannot afford to be without. When you get into risky investments, you risk excess money, not essential money. That is what the rich mean when they say you only play with play money.

**Betsy Broke:** My friends say only cowards are afraid of the stock market.

**Silver:** Yes, as Shakespeare said, cowards die many times before their time. And the reason they die is that they don't know what being brave is. When you are ignorant about something, and you don't know the rules of the game, so to speak, it is foolish to try to play the game whose rules you don't master. Consider your investment objectives.

There are four major financial phases in life:

1. A no-strings-attached youth,
2. Building a family,
3. Working towards retirement, and
4. Retirement itself.

Each phase affect your financial objectives differently. A phase 1 no-strings-attached youth can take much more risk than someone in phase 2 or phase 3. And ironically, someone who has had a good run and is in phase 4, can probably also handle more risk than someone in phase 2 or 3.

**Robbie Rich:** So, phase 2 and 3 is where one has to be more careful?

**Silver:** I would say more financially educated so that you can take calculated risks rather than carelessly throwing your money away. Risk is part of life and you have to take it. It is just better if you know what you are doing. You will be surprised, or not, that the rich who put money on the stock exchange, are not speculating. They bet on sure things, because they know the rules of the game.

**Betsy Broke:** But when you are in phase 2, for example, the demand on your time is huge. Where do you get the time to educate yourself?

**Silver:** Prioritise. You can follow Stephen

Covey[14]'s time matrix where time is divided into four quadrants.

You classify things as

| | |
|---|---|
| 1. Urgent and Important, | 2. Not urgent but important, |
| 3. Urgent but not Important, and | 4. Not urgent and not important. |

The things that will build your life are usually in quadrant 2: Not urgent but important. Education is almost always in this quadrant. All your time-wasters are things classified in quadrant 4: not urgent and not important. You shouldn't even be there at all. These include watching useless TV shows like a couch potato.

**Betsy Broke:** What about leisure time?

**Silver:** Genuine leisure time is guardant 2. Mindless chatter, however, is quadrant 4. You

---

[14] Read Steven R. Covey's books: First Things First, or The 7 Habits of Highly Effective People for more on the time matrix.

decide what is pleasurable.

**Robbie Rich:** So today I need to consider the four phases of life and the four quadrants of the time matrix, and figure out how much I can afford to lose, and what my priorities are.

# *23*

## **Acres Of Diamonds**

*"It is not so much where you are as what you are"*

Russel Conwell

Let's talk about a speech[15]. The Original motivational speech on Success. A speech that was delivered approximately 6000 times all over the United States of America. This speech made its owner a multimillionaire, but it also enriched the listeners, many of whom also became multimillionaires. (Could this happen to you if you heard the speech?)

---

15 *https://www.temple.edu/about/history-and-traditions/acres-diamonds*

Over 140 years ago, a Baptist minister, Russell Conwell, gave this speech. No, it was not a sermon; it was a speech on how to become wealthy. It became known as "Acres of Diamonds". It became perhaps the most famous speech of his era, 1870-1920. Of course, there was no commercial radio back then and hardly any movies. Speeches constituted both entertainment and education. While others went to theatre fro entertainment, others went to town halls and paid money to go and listen to a speech.

Conwell made so much money from this speech that he was able to build a hospital that later became a university. He supplied much of the initial funding of Temple University in Philadelphia. This is why Temple University keeps his speech on its website[16].

The speech is still in print. It still has readers. But

---

[16] *https://www.temple.edu/about/history-and-traditions/acres-diamonds*

overall, it is forgotten. The public no longer reads much, and we don't have much patience for speeches either. Other than a weekly sermon, the details of which are forgotten by evening, no other form of public speaking is familiar to modern adults today (unless you count political campaigning as speeches).

If you ever read the entire speech, you will be impressed by its irresistible quality. The main thrust of the speech was that *riches are right in your back yard*. It begins with an account of a storyteller on a boat in the Middle East who told of a rich man who sold his land and goods in order to go in search of diamonds. The man who bought his land found diamonds in the back yard.

He goes on to illustrate this point using others stories. The man who sold his land to go and look for gold in California, and gold was found in his own backyard. The man who sold his farm that had a river full of slush, to go and look for oil in Canada, only to have that slush turn out to be oil, found by the man who bought that land.

He talks of a professor of mineralogy who sold

his homestead, signing the deal sitting on a stone, to go and look for gold and silver, only to have that stone to be silver, discovered by the man who bought that homestead.

The speech's basic point needs to be learned by entrepreneurs in every generation. Most businesses are local. Most jobs are created by local businesses. Most millionaires made their money by starting a business and building it. The huge industries get the public's attention, but they are not the driving force of economic growth. Successful small businesses are.

Conwell further points out that the richest men of New York did not make their money in New York, but moved there after they made their money in small towns.

Conwell's point is simple: the entrepreneur should keep his attention on what his neighbours are buying or unable to buy. He further tells a story of a man, A.T. Stewart, who wanted to be rich and took all his money to go and buy a supply of needles, thread, and buttons, to come and sell to his neighbours, only to find that nobody needed needles, thread, and buttons.

He learned a great lesson, and from that day on, he decided he will ask his neighbours what they needed and he would sell only that which was in demand. That is how he became rich. An entrepreneur should search for niches in his town that are not being filled by high-quality sellers. Buyers want to be served, but they are having trouble getting decent services locally.

He states: "wherever there is a human need there is a greater fortune than a mine can furnish"

The best and brightest of our children have been sent to tertiary institutions by parents who do not understand that a standard B.A degree in liberal arts, while it may be interesting and important to the student, may not be nearly so lucrative in monetary terms as a certificate in plumbing or heating/air conditioning. The point is not that degrees are not important, but that certificates and diplomas that provide practical entrepreneurial courses are as important. Students who do certificates and diplomas should not be made to feel inferior to degree holders.

The examples that Conwell used to illustrate his point were what grabbed people's attention and, in some cases, their vision. He was a visionary. He was recruiting visionaries. People kept coming back over and over again to hear the speech. Those who heard it brought their friends and relatives to come and hear the speech. He was amazed by this.

While not everyone will become rich and most people are not sitting on oil fields or gold fields, no man is sitting in the midst of a world that has no needs to fill, no desires to placate, and no services to be rendered. There is a special something that a successful entrepreneur has, or at least had once, that the rest of us don't have. But, as Robert Kiyosaki, author of *Rich Dad Poor Dad*, says, we all have our share of self-doubt, but some more than others.

Part of the speech goes: "Love is the grandest thing on God's earth, but fortunate the lover who has plenty of money. Money is power: money has power; and for a man to say, 'I do not want money,' is to say 'I do not wish to do any good to my fellow men'. It is absurd thus to talk."

Conwell addresses entrepreneurs who are often trapped by the idea that they need capital to start anything. He says, "you don't need capital, you need common sense".

He asks, "Who are the great inventors? They are ever the simple, plain everyday people who see the need and set about to supply it."

He says "the man who made the greatest discoveries did it without any previous idea that he was an inventor".

He speaks of a carpenter who lost his job, and started a business by making wooden toys for his own children, and thus became one of the richest toy makers.

He speaks of a poor man who owned a maple tree and sat under it for forty years begging for survival, until a visitor suggested to him to make maple syrup from the sweet sap from that huge tree, and thus was born "rock maple crystal", and build a huge mansion by the side of that tree.

Everyone can make money. Everyone should make money. Everyone has been equipped in one way or another. Money is a tool. It is the most marketable commodity. Conwell was never trapped by the riches he generated. He gave away a fortune more than once. He build a hospital, that later became a university. You can't give money unless you have it. So generate it, then give it away. You can't just sit there and complain, besides, you may sitting and complaining while you're sitting on your own acres of diamonds.

# 24

## Your Money Behaviour

*"The time for action is now. It's never too late to do something."*
- Antoine de Saint-Exupery

Allow me to play the devil's advocate and sound the warning bell to watch your spending. You have to ask yourself why you let yourself be caught by the Christmas surprise every year. Christmas may only be a sign but not the cause. There may be many other events that catch you by surprise and throw your finances out of place. It may be a holiday season, a family event, a birthday, a celebration of some sorts. Every year you vow that next year it will be different, but every year it is the same old story.

Spending money wisely is part science, part art. Best case scenario, the ideal spender saves money off the top, fulfilling the "pay yourself first" rule, covers his or her basic needs, stays out of debt, gives generously to charity and gets real pleasure from planned, prudent purchases. If life was that easy, there would of course be no need for reminders such as this chapter or this book.

Based on the facts showing the rising consumer debt load all over the world, that isn't the case for many of us. Spenders can be out of control in countless ways. Some just fail to pay attention. The stingy are at war with their money. Others spend in hopes of finding self-esteem or social acceptance.

As Robert Kiyosaki states in his book, *The Cash Flow Quadrant*, some people solve financial problems by borrowing money. They even invest with borrowed money. Anything they own of value has debt attached to it. They think earning more money will solve their problems, but no matter how much money they make, they only get deeper into debt.

What kind of spender are you? Consider the following self-examination spending exercise designed to get you to think about how you spend money and, perhaps, to bring you closer to the ideal.

### When you receive your pay-cheque, do you:

- Have money skimmed off the top for your Retirement plan?
- and various pre-tax spending accounts for medical scheme?
- After which you then put money in regular savings and education accounts for the children?
- And then allocate what's left among your budget items, with discretionary items like entertainment at the bottom?
- Or do you pay off all the bills that have been piling up since your last paycheque and find there's nothing left?

### When you get a pay increase, you typically:

- Don't notice because your finances are so

tight anyway; or

- You go on a shopping spree; or
- Promise yourself again for the umpteenth time that you will draw up a workable budget; or
- You treat yourself to dinner out or some item you've been wanting and then allocate the rest to savings?

Or salary increases just never come your way?

Well, whatever your scenario, be sure to get in the habit of doing what you really want. Changes don't happen overnight. Don't wait until the opportune time to make your resolutions, start now, who knows, you might actually have a better year if you start planning now.

# 25

---

# Do You Feed Yourself Fully?

*"I want to know God's thoughts ...the rest are details."*
Albert Einstein.

**Silver:** At the beginning of each year, even if it be after a birthday when you'd be starting a new year in your age, or an anniversary, there is often a great question: What exactly am I going to do with this new year?

**Robbie Rich:** That's a great question, because every year we seem to be doing the same thing: making New Year resolutions, setting goals, trying to pursue them, but let's face it, the stuff does not work.

**Betsy Broke:** Perhaps instead of repeating the

history, we should try figure out a new approach.

**Silver:** Perhaps the way to go forward is to go backward. We need to go backwards and ask the all-important question: What has gone wrong?

**Robbie Rich:** Well, what do you think is going wrong? We must be doing something fundamentally wrong. How come we all start with great energy but by the third month it all dissipates and we are back into the rut?

**Silver:** It is simply because we work on the wrong stuff. We don't change our state of being. We keep worrying about the outcome, but not about the foundation.

**Robbie Rich:** Okay, let's lay the foundation again. What is the foundation?

**Silver:** We need to remember that at our core, we are more than our bodies. We actually have four bodies. We have the physical body, the mental body, the emotional body, and lastly, but my no means least, we have the spiritual or etheric body.

We are so often focussed on the physical body that we forget the other bodies that also need our attention. The physical body is the consumer, not the producer. It is also a tool that can used effectively by the other bodies if we paid attention.

The will does not come from the physical body alone, but from the synthesis of all four bodies. We get swept off our feet from our resolutions and goals by the third month because we don't have a strong will.

**Betsy Broke:** I think we are getting too esoteric here. So most of us live life at a physical body level; isn't that our primary identification? What is wrong with focusing on the physical body if it is all we can see ourselves as?

**Silver:** Very good points. We identify with the physical body, so life is about feeding the body, clothing the body, giving the body 'stuff'...

**Robbie Rich:** Nothing for the mind, nor for the emotions, nor for the spiritual bodies?

**Silver:** True. Most people haven't read a good book in ages. Think about the mental body: many people don't like to have to think. They would rather say: tell me what to do, where do I sit?

Where do I stand? What are the rules? What re the boundaries? Tell me, tell me, tell me – I'll do it! Tell me so I don't have to think!

**Robbie Rich:** Where did it go wrong?

**Silver:** It went wrong the moment we started ignoring the mental body, and the other bodies that we have. These, synthesized, are the greatest creative tools we have. We ignored them in favour of mindless television programs that are often addictive to our emotional body.

**Betsy Broke:** I guess it's time to make friends with, at least my mind again.

**Silver:** Indeed, it is time to read, to write poetry, to learn. It is time to observe and ask questions and seek real answers. It is time to stop agreeing with everything and start thinking of alternative answers and ways to do things.

**Betsy Broke:** We elect leaders so we don't have to think of solutions and we can just blame them.

**Silver:** By so doing we have relinquished responsibility. So we become couch potatoes even of our own lives. It is time to start the year with a thinking program. Feed the mind please!

Contemplate your emotional needs. Consider your spiritual needs. Read good books – books that will make you think and feel deeply about real life, not addictive emotional soap operas.

**Robbie Rich:** Are we saying that things in my life are going wrong because I have neglected my Real Self?

**Betsy Broke:** Well, who's solutions are we trying to implement in our own lives? Those that we thought of ourselves or suggestions from others?

**Silver:** Mindlessly trying to implement other people' solutions is often like trying to hammer a square peg into a round hole. Taking responsibility includes thinking of solutions ourselves, and if they fail, we have no one to blame, but, we shall have learnt a whole lot more from the process. That can only lead to growth.

If these ideas sound strange, then maybe it's time to research them, and then come up with your own conclusions, instead of constantly living off of the opinions of others.

## *Reader Comments*

*Thank you very much Sir for your article titled "Conquer Fear", which appeared in the Botswana Guardian dated 15 July 2005. S.P.*

\*\*

*My man, (in reference to your article "Conquer Fear"), No please don't conquer fear. If you do you shall subdue it. It will surface and you shall be prone to all problems and difficulties of life. So... be afraid and know that you feel fear because that way you shall be jolted to your best abilities and use your potential to the best. CPL.*

# 26

---

# Food for Thought

*"Man is buffeted by circumstance so long as he believed himself to be the creature of outside conditions."*
James Allen.

**Betsy Broke:** It is one thing to say let's feed the mind. It is another to actually find the good books that one can read. Where would be a great place to start reading?

**Silver:** Well, for starters, I think joining a book club could be a great place to start. If there is no book club to join, perhaps you should invite a few friends to start one. To actually say what is a great book would be a very subjective thing. Each person is interested by different subjects and your mind will be stimulated by certain subjects, while others may lull you to sleep.

**Betsy Broke:** You are not about to say that I should abandon reading novels right?

**Silver:** There are actually great works of fiction that could get your mind thinking. Science fiction, for example, could get you wondering in galaxies you never knew existed. But it is important to also be aware that there are addictive emotional books that will do nothing to grow you, but rather will pull you down into the pit of human emotions, and drag you to abuse your human energies.

**Robbie Rich:** While we are focused in this discussion in the field of personal finance and personal development, where could we start in terms of great books?

**Silver:** Well, I think a good place to start feeding the mind would be books about how the mind functions. What I think are good books include John Kehoe's book, *Mind Power Into the 21st Century*; Napoleon Hill's *Think and Grow Rich*; And, if you have the stomach for it, Neal Walsch's *Conversations with God* series. A book you could start with is written by Dr. Joseph Murphy, and is called *The Power of The Subconscious Mind.*

**Robbie Rich:** What is that about?

**Silver:** It is a book that explains the power of the subconscious mind and how you can actively use your mind to create anything that you want in your life.

**Betsy Broke:** Why would Neal Walsch's Conversation with God series need guts?

**Silver:** Because most of us are afraid of the idea that God could actually talk to us one on one. Much less just answer our daily questions.

**Betsy Broke:** So what is the main thrust of The Power of the Subconscious Mind book by Dr Murphy?

**Silver:** Remember most people will not get the same thrust our of the same book. But, like Think and Grow Rich, it goes into details to explain that if you don't actively make a decision to Think and Grow Rich, you are probably Thinking and Growing Poor by default.

**Robbie Rich:** You mean that my subconscious mind creates my reality with or without my knowledge or involvement?

**Silver:** Something like that. You are actually more involved than you would realise. It urges you to take control of your life instead of letting it go with the flow. Many people go with the flow precisely because of what we talked about earlier. They don't want to think. They just want to be told what to do.

**Betsy Broke:** I guess there is a true danger in not setting the course for your life, and letting it be determined by the circumstances of life.

**Robbie Rich:** Aren't we just saying we should get back to setting goals? New Year resolutions and the like?

**Silver:** It is one thing to just set goals, it is entirely another to ensure that they get fulfilled. Goals set and left to chance will not happen. But if you know the rules of the game, so to speak, then you understand and know where the game is going. You can asses whether you are making progress or not, and you can change course if you find that you are on the wrong direction.

**Betsy Broke:** So do these kinds of books really

work? These Think and Grow Rich type books?

**Silver:** Everything works if you work it. Most of these books that we are discussing today have practical exercises that if followed, can lead to real change in your life. There are also workbooks available that can help to spell the process out and you can set your goals and actually see the changes within.

**Robbie Rich:** I guess such books advocate internal change instead of just external change.

**Silver:** Exactly. When your attitude is different, you start to see the world differently. Obstacles become opportunities, and failure can be turned into success easily.

# 27

---

# Where there's a Will, there's a Way

*"My chief want in life is someone who shall make me do what I can."*
Ralph Waldo Emerson

---

**Silver:** In a short survey[17] we carried out involving a sample of people of whom over 60% have a university degree and above, a whopping 88% did not have a will drawn up!

**Robbie Rich:** I think a will is a thing that can easily be postponed, because it never seems to have the pressure of urgency, and yet it is such

---

[17] Nelson Letshwene, *Personal Financial Management in Botswana – a study*. UNISA

an important document.

**Silver:** You need to realise that not drawing a will or doing a proper estate planning does not necessarily inconvenience you, but it definitely will inconvenience your beneficiaries after your death.

**Robbie Rich:** I think most of us, or rather speaking for myself, I think I don't have enough stuff to warrant a will.

**Betsy Broke:** You'll be surprised what people fight over after death. They will fight over your shirt or shoe. And I don't think it's the shoe or the shirt that's important, it is the idea of holding on to some portion of you.

**Silver:** If you love your family, (there's that guilt inducing statement often used by insurance agents), take some time now and draw up a will or do proper estate planning. That statement should actually read: if you love yourself, then draw up a will. That's because all we do is really for ourselves. The will is a means of control that you give to yourself. It keeps on 'deciding' for you even when you are not physically present to decide. It is like sending your controlling power into your unforeseeable future.

**Betsy Broke:** That puts a nice ring to it. Continuing to exercise control even over the little that you have.

**Silver:** No matter how hard you work and how much you save, if you can't bother to write a will so that you can control your wealth and protect your beneficiaries after you are gone, you are still leaving them to the mercy of the court systems, the tired judges and magistrates who will appoint their own friends as executors of your estate and share in the plunder.

**Robbie Rich:** Are you saying the system is flawed?

**Silver:** Not having a will is leaving your estate to be distributed by someone who never knew you nor cared about your beneficiaries, and he will distribute your wealth as he sees fit. I guess if you did not bother to decide what you want happening to your wealth by writing a will, the judge may be right in assuming that you did not care!

**Betsy Broke:** Talking about a will is like pre-empting death to some people. It's like saying you are about to die.

**Robbie Rich:** A mention of the word, 'will', gets people to run into a defensive denial state of, 'who said I'm going to die?'

**Silver:** Well, hello! Everyone dies! But not everyone really lives. (Remember that line from the movie *"Brave-heart"* spoken by William Wallace (Mel Gibson)?)

**Robbie Rich:** The problem with death is that it doesn't announce and give you a chance to set your house in order.

**Silver:** Well, for that very reason, it's time to stop the denial of your physical mortality and just face the music. Fire up that will and get it over and done with. Drawing a will is actually an opportunity.

Betsy Broke: An opportunity?

**Silver:** It gives you an opportunity to think what you would like your life to mean to those who are left behind.

**Betsy Broke:** But I think it's also an opportunity

to tidy things up. Maybe your things are all over the place and people might not know where to find what.

**Robbie Rich:** You also get to give final instructions of your life. No one can argue with your will if it's a valid will.

**Silver:** The legacy you leave will depends on the plan you prepare. Through careful thought and use of the proper tools, you can leave your beneficiaries the estate you always meant for them to have. Developing your estate plan is a personal process. It is part of a comprehensive financial plan that is grounded in the attitudes, beliefs and traditions that you consider important.

**Robbie Rich**: I guess you might have to think of naming a guardian for your children?

**Silver:** If you don't want your children scattered all over the country among your relatives, it is best you name a guardian in your will. This way you can make sure the guardian is someone that your children will be comfortable with, and you can also make provision for them to have some of your wealth to raise your kids.

**Betsy Broke:** What are the other things to think about when you write a will?

**Silver:** Further question to consider include: Do you have current powers of attorney covering both health and financial issues? Do you have a living will (medical directive) regarding life support in the event of a dire medical prognosis?

Nearly everyone—from the wealthy to those of very modest means—can benefit from a well-designed estate plan. So, just do it.

# 28

## Do You Have a Definite Purpose?

*"Both Poverty and Riches are the Offspring of thought"*
Napoleon Hill.

Let's take one idea from Napoleon Hill's book, Think and Grow Rich, and discuss it. One of the ideas that runs as a strong point of most of Napoleon Hill's books, including The Law of Success, is that to succeed in life, you must have a definite chief purpose in your life.

**Betsy Broke:** Isn't that the same as setting New Year resolutions, or goals as we discussed before?

**Silver:** Not really. As you know, most New Year resolutions stem from a wishful thinking and most people don't really think deeply about their impact. In the past we emphasised the importance of taking time to set your goals and getting them embedded into your life.

**Robbie Rich:** A definite Chief Purpose is more like your mission in this life. You have to ask yourself that important question: Why am I here.

**Silver:** Exactly.

**Betsy Broke:** But that's too scary. I'll have to think hard to get answers to that question.

**Silver:** Would you rather just go with the flow aimlessly? The quickest way to deal with purpose is actually to ask yourself: Who Am I?

**Betsy Broke**: Who Am I? What kind of a question is that?

**Silver:** Good Question. As you approach each situation or event or person in life, ask yourself that question: Who Am I in relation to this? When you meet poverty, you ask yourself, Who Am I in relation to this? Am I a giver or one who stands in judgement? Do I get involved or do I stay aloof?

**Betsy Broke:** I can see how that can go a long way in helping me to define and recreate myself in every situation.

**Silver:** Every act is an act of self-definition.

**Robbie Rich:** Well, most of us are detached from what we believe is our purpose in life. We are employed and we end up doing a job just because it will pay the bills, and meanwhile we burry our talents and hope that someday in the future, we will find time to pursue our real mission in life.

**Silver:** Do you imagine that the bills will one day stop coming, and then suddenly you will be free to pursue your purpose?

**Robbie Rich:** That is an illusion. So, what should I do right now to pursue my real purpose in life? Do I just drop everything and start pursuing it?

**Silver:** No, That would be going from one misery to another. You need to have an exit plan from your current state to your desired state. For most of us, the plan will include two main categories: A Debt Elimination Plan, and a Wealth Creation

Strategy.

**Betsy Broke:** We have already talked about a Debt Elimination Plan.

**Silver:** And over the course of this discussion, we have been talking about the Wealth Creation Strategy, perhaps in less specific terms.

**Robbie Rich:** So, what is missing?

**Silver:** The will and the application. So here goes what you could do to start with. Account for where you are right now by doing your basic financial statements, then set some SMART goals.

**Betsy Broke:** What are SMART goals?

**Silver:** SMART is an acronym for:

**S**pecific – not vague, identifiable

**M**easurable – by time or by money or some yardstick

**A**chievable – not a pie in the sky

**R**ealistic – not fantasyland goals, but dream big enough for you.

**T**imely – can be achieved within a particular time frame

Take an example: if say your goal is to gross one million bucks in one year, then,

*Specific*: one million in one year

*Measurable*: This means 83,333.33 per month

*Achievable*: If your products are say 100.00 each, this means 833 items per month, or 208 items per week or about 42 items per day.

*Realistic*: Based on your history and your capability, you have to ask yourself if this is realistic in your industry

*Timely*: Can this goal be achieved within one year or six months, or do you need 2 years, to be realistic?

The big idea is to get you out of debt and get you started on building your financial wealth account, so that you can jump off the train going the wrong way with you, and pursue your purpose.

**Robbie Rich:** That means, in the short term, my purpose is to focus on a plan that will get me out of 'the rat race', so that I can get onto the 'fast track'.

# 29

## Can You Develop Self-Confidence?

*"Skepticism is the deadly enemy of progress and self-development"*
Napoleon Hill.

Napoleon Hill writes in *The Law of Success*: "The development of self-confidence starts with the elimination of this demon called fear, which sits on a man's shoulder and whispers to him: 'You can't do it – you are afraid to try – you are afraid of public opinion – you are afraid that you will fail – you are afraid that you have not the ability'"

**Betsy Broke:** That is a very interesting quotation

because I find that it applies directly to me. I have had so many brilliant ideas that I ended up shelving because of exactly that very voice of fear. Why is it that we let our fears stop us?

**Silver:** It is because of the wrong perception you have of yourself. Most of us don't look at ourselves primarily through our own eyes. We always see ourselves through the eyes and opinion of others. We seek uniformity and conformity instead of our true unique self.

**Betsy Broke:** Are you saying that I should ignore other people's opinions about myself?

**Silver:** In as far as you perceive them to be putting you down, I think yes you should completely ignore them. Only as they lift you up and encourage you to pursue your goals, then can you allow them in.

**Betsy Broke:** Well, how do I know which opinions to accept and which to discard? I don't want to ignore warnings. Perhaps someone is genuinely trying to save me from trouble.

**Silver:** You can tell whether an opinion is motivated by fear or by love. Those who have walked a path will never discourage you from walking your own chosen path; instead they will guide you and encourage you. They know that experience is your best teacher and they will never take this away from you by dissuading you. Fear comes mostly from those who have never tried.

**Betsy Broke:** So I will know from within.

**Silver:** Yes. Self-Confidence comes from within, from the Self. It is not called Others-Confidence. If you keep looking for it from others, you will never find it. Think about one of those brilliant ideas that you discarded. Which of your friends had tried any of them?

**Betsy Broke:** But you are always told, you won't get funding or support or clients.

**Silver:** Perhaps start on a small scale. Anything that comes from The Labour of Love principle is bound to succeed.

**Betsy Broke:** What is the Labour of Love principle?

**Silver:** Anything that you love so much that you will be prepared to do even without pay or with minimal pay, will eventually grow. Only three things you will have to do: Shut down the voice of doubt from within, surround yourself with encouraging people, and keep dreaming big dreams.

**Betsy Broke:** And one more thing, remember that Self-Confidence is confidence in the Self, and is from the Self.

**Silver:** And remember that you are unique. There is no one else on the planet like you, and your offerings can therefore never be exactly like those of anybody else.

# *30*

## Acquire Specialized Knowledge

*"Knowledge will not attract money unless it is organised and intelligently directed through practical plans of action to the definite end ..."*
Napoleon Hill.

One of the keys of success as written about by Napoleon Hill in his *The Law of Success* and *Think and Grow Rich* is the acquisition of specialised knowledge and the organisation of such knowledge to a definite end.

**Robbie Rich:** Are we now talking about pursuing your profession and trying to excel in it?

**Silver:** The only problem with our educational institutions is that they pump so much general knowledge into students that at the end most students don't know what to do with such knowledge. What Napoleon Hill is writing about is that knowledge should be organised and used for specific purpose. He writes: "The word 'educate' is derived from the Latin word 'educo', meaning to draw out, or to develop from within... An educated man is not necessarily one who has an abundance of general or specialised knowledge, ... but one who has so developed the faculties of his mind that he may acquire anything he wants, or its equivalent, without violating the rights of others"

**Robbie Rich:** It seems we are talking here about the application of knowledge.

**Silver:** That is exactly it. Wisdom is the application of knowledge. Wisdom comes from critical thinking on the data that knowledge is. Knowledge is really a body of raw data. Once that data is organised in an intelligent way, it can be useful and once that intelligence is applied, you have wisdom.

**Robbie Rich:** I see that being wise is really being

able to apply knowledge. How can I start my own business based only on my profession?

**Betsy Broke:** If say you are a plumber and you want to start your own business, don't you necessarily have to acquire all the other skills needed to run a business?

**Silver:** That is exactly where cooperation with others comes in. The problem with people who now believe they have to know everything is that they will limit themselves. It is impossible to know everything. We live in the information age and our access to information is doubling almost every year. There are new accounting skills, new marketing strategies, new ways to deal with employees, and of course new plumbing systems for your plumbing business. The fourth industrial revolution is upon us.

**Robbie Rich:** So I need to learn to outsource my non-core business and focus on my plumbing?

**Silver:** That is why we talk of forming a Mastermind group. In a mastermind group, you can have a lawyer, an accountant, a marketer, an engineer, and any other specialised knowledge.

Everyone expands their field of expertise and everyone's business benefits.

**Robbie Rich:** So most of us fail because we try to do it all?

**Silver:** Yes, it is impossible to do it all. It is also difficult to succeed if you are independent, or too dependent. Interdependence is the way to go. A dependent person is one who relies almost entirely on others. He is prone to blame-shifting. An independent person is very self-reliant. He is prone to fatigue. An interdependent person is the smart one. He is prone to fulfilment and achievement. You choose who you would rather be. If all the specialised people give business to each other with respect, then all will be developed because all the specialised knowledge is needed in just about every business, whether big or small.

**Robbie Rich:** So the formations of Mastermind groups should be the answer to business growth. At each meeting one person from one profession could make a presentation to the others just to inform them of the latest things that will affect their businesses. That is brilliant. When do we start?

**Silver:** You can start anytime anywhere. In each town there could be a Mastermind group formed by business people in the town. All it takes is one person to organise one. Will you be the one?

**Robbie Rich:** If not me then who?

**Silver:** Indeed!

# 31

---

# Do You Need A mentor or A Coach?

*"Success requires no explanations, failure permits no alibis."*

Napoleon Hill.

**Robbie Rich:** Some people believe you should have a mentor to help you out. But I also hear of coaching, what is the difference between a mentor and a coach?

**Silver:** The answer could lead to an academic debate, but people don't often realise that there is a difference between a mentor and a coach. I will give a lose definition of each. A mentor is an experienced and trusted advisor, while a coach is one who gives hints.

**Robbie Rich:** If I am running a business, what do I need – a mentor or a coach?

**Silver:** Your needs can only be determined by yourself and your situation. A mentor is by definition, an experienced and trusted advisor. I think a lot of people already understand that mentoring is a one-to-one process, while coaching can be a process of helping you to get the best out of you. Let me ask you this, if you are a soccer star, do you need a mentor or a coach?

**Robbie Rich:** Everybody knows I need a coach.

**Silver:** Well, you may actually need a bit of both, but it is perceived that you need a coach because you already have the talent. As a talented star, what you need is someone to help you get the most out of your own talent, and coordinate it with other talents on the field. In other words, a coach will not give you soccer talent; they will only help you to grow the one you already have.

**Robbie Rich:** I see, but a mentor on the other hand is someone who could give me the skills? It is someone who has helped me one-on-one to develop the talent that I have?

**Silver:** That's correct. That is why part of the definition of a mentor mentions trust. Not that a coach does not need to be trusted. Coaching may therefore loosely be defined as suitable for a team. A coach is one who will coordinate the talents of your team.

**Robbie Rich:** So, in my business, do I need a mentor or a coach?

**Silver:** If you have been running businesses before, you probably only need a coach. A coach does not need to know the specifics of your industry, but their job is to come in, understand what you are trying to do and give you the best possible routes to your destination. You could also get mentors in specific areas.

**Robbie Rich:** So if I am making a lot of money and I need to invest it, all I need is an investment mentor?

**Silver:** Absolutely. A mentor is one who is playing a better bigger game. You don't need a coach there, you need an investment mentor –

someone whom you trust, and is experienced in that field. If the rest of your business is okay, that is, production is going well, people are happy, but the sales and marketing is not going well, what your marketing team may need may be a marketing coach. But if it is just for you, then it may be a marketing mentor.

So the easiest distinction will be that a mentor is one who works in-depth one-on-one, while a coach is one who works in-depth with the team.

**Robbie Rich:** That is why you say I could have several mentors in different areas. That means I must be able to identify the specific area in which I need help, and I must identify someone I can trust in the field and get them to come and help me.

**Silver:** Yes, a soccer coach, for example, can work with many talented people on the field. He helps them to coordinate their different talents for one objective. A business coach can work with your entire organisation, coordinating the different talents you have in your business towards your objectives. But I think it is best if you choose your own mentors – people you trust.

## Reader Comment

*Nelson, I read your article with great enthusiasm. Please keep up the good work of keeping us informed!!!*

*Regards, CNC.*

# *32*

## Wealth-Building Secrets Of The Richest Man In Babylon

*"Learn from yesterday, live for today, hope for tomorrow."*

-Albert Einstein

**Silver:** One of the most important tools in increasing financial capability is to read. Today I would like us to go through one of the books I always recommend for people to read.

**Robbie Rich**: You have recommended many books including The Money Field, Seven Essential Money Skills, Think and Grow Rich and others.

**Silver:** Today's book is: "*The Richest Man in*

*Babylon*" by George S. Clason. We will highlight some of the important wealth-building principles articulated there.

**Betsy Broke:** Do these principles work in real life for certain?

**Silver:** In my quest to search for principles that make sense, in the spirit of Napoleon Hill who studied hundreds of millionaires to search for insights, I do recommend these and urge those who dare to try, to go ahead. They work if you put them into practice.

**Robbie Rich:** Let's get into it.

**Silver:** Babylon was reputed to be the wealthiest city of the ancient world. Not just in terms of its ruling class, but also among a large population of merchants and professionals and farmers who lived in beautiful homes, enjoyed produce from their own gardens, and were able to comfortably retire well before they were too old to work.

**Robbie Rich:** Is this book a historical record of what happened in Babylon?

**Silver:** I don't think so. I think the book uses parables from Babylon to teach lessons. It's not a serious book, but it's an amusing read if you have a taste for success parables. It's also a reminder of the wealth-building principles in the tradition of Ben Franklin and Napoleon Hill's millionaires in "*Think and Grow Rich*".

The story begins with Bansir, "sitting upon the low wall surrounding his property, gazing sadly at his simple home and the open workshop in which stood a partially completed chariot."

Kobbi, a friend and musician, stops by to borrow two shekels.

> "If I had two shekels," Bansir replies gloomily, "to no one could I lend them -- not even to you, my best of friends; for they would be my fortune. No one lends his entire fortune, not even to a best friend."

Floored by the thought that the two of them haven't got two shekels between them, the old friends begin to speculate on the disparity of wealth in Babylon, even among free men, and cannot understand why they, who have worked so hard for so many years, are still so poor.

**Robbie Rich:** I can see how most of us could relate to such a story. Many of us work hard for years and still end up broke.

**Silver:** They decide to consult with Arkad, who is said to be the richest man in Babylon. Estern wisdom says, if you want to know the road to the mountain, ask the person who goes up and down that mountain.

> "So rich [is Arkad] the king is said to seek his golden aid in affairs of the treasury," Kobbi says.
>
> "So rich," Bansir interrupts, "that I fear if I should meet him in the darkness of the night, I should lay my hands upon his fat wallet."
>
> "Nonsense," says Kobbi. "A man's wealth is not in the purse he carries. A fat purse quickly empties if there be no golden stream to refill it. Arkad has an income that constantly keeps his purse full, no matter how liberally he spends."

> "Income -- that is the thing," exclaims Bansir. "I wish an income that will keep flowing into my purse whether I sit upon the wall or travel to far lands."

And with that goal in mind, the two old friends go to seek the wisdom of Arkad.

Thus ends the first chapter of "The Richest Man in Babylon," with Basir coming to an important understanding:

> "The reason why we have never found any measure of wealth," he says, "is because we never sought it."

In the second chapter we meet Arkad, "far and wide famed for his great wealth. He was generous in his charities . . . with his family . . . in his own expenses . . . but nevertheless each year his wealth increased more rapidly than he spent it."

[If you have already read through the book, I still believe that this summary will help you in putting into action some of the things you may have learnt.]

Bansir and Kobbi are not the only wealth seekers asking for Arkad's help. Some of them, "friends of younger days," question why fate has singled him out "to enjoy all the good things of life and ignore us who are equally deserving."

"Once we were equal," they point out. "We studied under the same master. We played in the same games. And in neither the studies nor the games did you outshine us. And in the years since, you have been no more honourable a citizen than we. Nor have you worked harder or more faithfully."

Arkad says, "If you have not acquired more than a bare existence in the years since we were youths, it is because you either have failed to learn the laws that govern the building of wealth or else you do not observe them."

Arkad is stating that building wealth follows laws. If you break these laws you won't make it, and if you observe these laws, you will make it. Would you say you know these laws?

**Betsy Broke:** We probably know the laws, but maybe it's hard to follow them?

**Silver:** Arkad states that the desire to have all of these good things was not enough. It was not until he learned a lesson about wealth building from his mentor, Algamish, that his fortune changed.

> Algamish told him, "I found the road to wealth when I decided that a part of all I earned was mine to keep. And so will you."
>
> "But all I earn is mine to keep, is it not?" Arkad demanded.
>
> "Far from it," Algamish replied. "Do you not pay the garment maker? Do you not pay the sandal maker? Do you not pay for the things you eat? Can you live in Babylon without spending? What have you to show for your earnings of the past month? What for the past year? Fool! You pay to everyone but yourself. Dullard, you

labour for others. As well be a slave and work for what your master gives you to eat and wear. If you did keep for yourself one-tenth of all you earn, how much would you have in 10 years?"

"As much as I earn in one year," Arkad replied.

"You speak but half the truth," Algamish retorted. "Every gold piece you save is a slave to work for you. Every copper it earns is its child that also can earn for you. If you would become wealthy, then what you save must earn, and its children must earn, that all may help to give to you the abundance you crave.

"Wealth, like a tree, grows from a tiny seed. The first copper you save is the seed from which your tree of wealth shall grow. The sooner you plant that seed, the sooner shall the tree grow. And the more faithfully you nourish and water that tree with consistent savings, the sooner may you bask in contentment beneath its shade."

And that was the beginning of Arkad's journey to wealth.

**Robbie Rich:** It's a very simple idea. The money you spend on the trappings of wealth - cars, jewellery, etc. - may make you feel wealthy, but they don't add to your wealth; they subtract from it.

**Silver:** If you want to increase your wealth, there is only one way to do that: You must save. And if you want to save regularly and well, you should put a portion of your income into savings first -- before you spend it on anything else.

**Betsy Broke:** Making the conversion from a spender to a saver isn't easy. It takes more than simply reading this and saying to yourself, "Yes, that's true. I know that."

**Robbie Rich:** It takes commitment and the discipline to follow a carefully articulated savings-and-investment plan over time.

**Silver:** The first thing you need to do is decide how much of your income you will "pay to yourself first." That number, as Clason suggests, should be at least one-tenth of your income and can be "as much as you are comfortable with."

And it has to be done consistently with each and every paycheque and every time you bring in any extra income.

> "If I set for myself a task," Arkad says, "I shall see it through. ... Therefore, I am careful not to start difficult and impractical tasks, because I love leisure."

That is a profoundly important point. You want to make "paying yourself first" a regular habit -- because until it becomes a habit, it is a chore.

**Betsy Broke:** But why save money when there are pressing needs in front of you?

**Silver:** The purpose of wealth building is not the acquisition of wealth itself but the power and peace of mind it can bring you. Unless and until you make paying yourself first an automatic part of your day-to-day routine, you won't enjoy those benefits.

**Robbie Rich:** It's easy to see why many people arrive at middle age without a shekel in their pocket. They have worked long and hard in various professions and at times have enjoyed incomes well above average. But their personal balance sheet has a negative net-worth.

**Silver:** We are all apportioned an equal number of hours in every day and, over our lifetimes, different opportunities. The trick to overcoming the misfortune of fortune is, as Algamish taught Arkad, to begin by paying yourself first.

So here goes our action plan for today: Starting right now, you're going to "pay yourself first." Here's how:

- Start, immediately, by banking at least one-tenth of your gross (not net) income.

- If this means you can't pay the other people in your life (the landlord, the grocer, etc.), find a second stream of income and/or reduce your spending.

- Be sure to save at least 10% of that second stream of income too.

- Don't give yourself any breaks. Don't make any excuses. Pay yourself first. Stick with the plan.

- Consider that pool of money to be your

wealth. Don't count any value you have in your car, house, and toys. Each month, take a measure of that pool. Make sure it is deeper than it was the month before.

# 33

---

# The Value Of Expert Advice

*"Nothing stops the man who desires to achieve. Every obstacle is simply a course to develop his achievement muscle. It's a strengthening of his powers of accomplishment."*

Thomas Carlyle on Obstacles

**Silver:** As we said earlier, it's almost impossible to build wealth unless you develop the habit of saving. And to do that, you have to "pay yourself first." That's the lesson Bansir and Kobbi learned from Akard in the second chapter of "The Richest Man in Babylon". But then Akard goes on to explain to them why, though it is important, saving is not, by itself, enough to make you rich. He continues with his story:

"I thought about what [Algamish] had said to me, and it seemed reasonable. So I decided that I would try it. Each time I was paid, I took one from each ten pieces of copper and hid it away. And strange as it may seem, I was no shorter of funds than before. I noticed little difference as I managed to get along without it...

> "A twelfth month after Algamish had gone, he again returned and said to me, 'Son, have you paid to yourself not less than one-tenth of all you have earned this past year?"
>
> Akard answered proudly, "Yes, master. I have."
>
> "That is good," said Algamish. "And what have you done with it?"
>
> "I have given it to Azmur, the brick maker, who told me he was travelling over the far seas and in Tyre he would buy for me the rare jewels of the Phoenicians. When he returns, we shall sell these at high prices and divide the earnings."

"Every fool must learn," Algamish growled. "But *why trust the knowledge of a brick maker about jewels*? Would you go to the bread maker to inquire about the stars? No, you would go to the astrologer, if you had the power to think. Your savings are gone, youth. You have jerked your wealth tree up by the roots. But plant another. Try again. And next time if you would have the advice about jewels, go to the jewel merchant. If you would know the truth about sheep, go to the herdsman. Advice is one thing that is freely given away, but watch that you take only what is worth having. He who takes advice about his savings from one who is inexperienced in such matters shall pay with his savings."

So saying, Algamish went away.

**Robbie Rich:** That is a profound lesson. That is how many of us lose money that we invest, by getting wrong advice from people who know nothing about investing.

**Silver:** I'm sure you've witnessed Akard's sad story more times than you'd like to admit. Some people are separated from their money as the result of falling victim to cheating, lying, and other sorts of knavery. But all are guilty themselves of making some form of the stupid mistake Akard made during his early attempt to become wealthy: taking moneymaking advice from someone who didn't actually know anything about it. It's astounding how many people do that.

**Robbie Rich:** There are many self-proclaimed investment experts . . . and even government-authorized financial experts, for that matter . . . who don't necessarily know what they are talking about.

**Silver:** Brokers must pass a battery of tests before they can start selling stocks or shares, but none of those exams can predict how seriously they will study the stocks they recommend or how well those stocks will perform in the free market.

Although some investment experts do have substantial and impressive track records, many more do not.

**Betsy Broke:** As Arkad learned, we need expert advice . . . but how do we get it?

**Silver:** First, recognize the difference between investing and wealth building.

**Robbie Rich:** Wait a minute. We're talking about saving. Now we're onto investing, and wealth building. It seems that there are three topics?

**Silver:** It starts with a commitment to "pay yourself first", that is saving. Investing is giving your money a chance to grow. Wealth building is your ability to keep your money, and ensure that it keeps working for you.

**Betsy Broke:** Everyone can do the first step. When it comes to the other steps, you will need expert advice.

**Silver:** In the book, *Seven Essential Money Skills*[18], the author emphasises that everyone can learn these skills if they commit to it. That book makes a distinction between earning money,

---

[18] R Nelson Letshwene, 2015, Seven Essential Money Skills, Moedi Publishing, also available on amazon.com in digital format (kindle) and paperback format.

saving money, investing money, and building value.

Michael Masterson, author of *Automatic Wealth*, points out in his e-letter, ETR: "The interesting thing about the world of financial advice is that the more valuable the advice is, the less you are usually asked to pay for it... The really invigorating knowledge -- the profoundest truths and most powerful secrets -- are available almost free to all who want them."

These are the time-tested, experience-proven truths that great books from Aristotle's "Poetics" to Ben Franklin's "Poor Richard's Almanac" to "The Richest Man in Babylon" have in common.

**Betsy Broke:** It seems that one of the investments I must focus on is acquiring great books so that I have access to great knowledge.

Silver: That is true. Make wealth building your goal and develop a detailed plan to achieve it. Keep a part of what you earn. Get advice from people who truly know what they're talking about. This sort of advice is what you get when you speak to people who have a lifetime of financial success behind them. Ask them a question about how they became so successful and they will usually give you an answer that sounds rather ordinary.

**Robbie Rich:** But we often think it should be so complicated.

**Silver:** So, back to the question: How do you get good wealth-building advice?

1. Shun the advice of amateurs - friends, family members, and the like. Take their advice only in subjects where they have proven themselves to be experienced.

2. Be wary of commissioned salespeople. A person whose compensation is tied to how much you invest, not how much you profit, needs to be engaged with care. Trust them if they are upfront about their commission and are not trying to hide that fact. Knowing how much you are paying them, you can measure the value of their service to you.

3. Don't go back and forth between advisers.

Find one who is willing to give his best secrets free. Make sure those secrets make sense to you, then pay him well. Examine his track record for making recommendations. Commit only a small portion of your savings to his care until you have confidence in him -- and even then, increase the amount you put in his hands slowly. But remember, he is not responsible for your losses any more than he is responsible for your wins. You take full responsibility for your actions. It is your decision to put your money with him, he will not force you to.

## *34*

---

# The Five Laws Of Gold from –
# The Richest Man in Babylon

*"Gold is reserved for those who know its laws and*
*abide by them,"*
George S Clason

**Robbie Rich:** I think the idea of discussing a book like we're doing with *The Richest Man in Babylon*, is very helpful in getting us to discuss the important points.

**Betsy Broke:** Perhaps as people we could form groups wherever we live and pick one book, read it together and discuss what we're each learning from the book.

**Silver:** Lack of education is the greatest impediment to the wealth of a nation and an ignorance of the fundamentals of wealth building is the biggest reason for personal poverty. Taking short cuts is another.

Robbie Rich: It was Stephen Covey in "*The Seven habits of highly effective people*", who said those who cram their way through tertiary education – goofing off during the term and then sitting down to cram for the exam - end up getting the degree but not the education.

**Silver:** That was precisely the conclusion that the King and his Chancellor came to in the third chapter of "The Richest Man in Babylon."

> "Where is all the gold that we spent for these great improvements?" demanded the King.
>
> "It has found its way, I fear," responded the Chancellor, "into the possession of a few very rich men of our city. It filtered through the fingers of most of our people as quickly as the goat's milk goes through the strainer. Now that the stream of gold

has ceased to flow, most of our people have nothing to show for their earnings."

"Why should so few men be able to acquire all the gold?" the King asked.

"Because they know how," replied the Chancellor. "One may not condemn a man for succeeding because he knows how. Neither may one with justice take away from a man what he has fairly earned, to give to men of less ability."

"But why," demanded the king, "should not all the people learn how to accumulate gold and therefore become themselves rich and prosperous?"

"Quite possible, Your Excellency. But who can teach them?"

"Who knows best in all our city how to become wealthy?" the King asked.

"Thy question answers itself," the Chancellor said. "It must be the man who has amassed the greatest wealth in Babylon."

And so it was that Arkad was summoned before

the King, who interrogated him about his success. He discovered that Arkad had not begun with anything that anyone else didn't have, including "a great desire for wealth."

Since it was the King's desire for all Babylonians to know how to become wealthy, Arkad promised to teach all that he knew to 100 men.

> "I will teach them those seven cures that did fatten my purse, one that was once as lean as any in Babylon."

> > (I wrote about these seven cures in the March 26th edition of the Guardian – please find a copy and review). What I will discuss here is another Lesson that Arkad taught his students. The five laws of gold.

What Is Worth More Than Gold? "A bag heavy with gold or a clay tablet carved with words of wisdom: If thou had thy choice, which wouldst thou choose?" That was the question Old Kalabab asked his students, wealth seekers who had come to ask his advice. And how did the wealth seekers respond? "The gold! The gold!" they shouted.

"So it is with the sons of men," rued Kalabab. "Give them a choice of gold and wisdom and they will ignore the wisdom and waste the gold."

Alas! Human nature is weak. "Gold is reserved for those who know its laws and abide by them," Old Kalabab said. And to illustrate this truth, he told the tale of his master, Nomasir, the son of Arkad (the richest man in Babylon).

"In Babylon," Kalabab began, "it is the custom that the sons of wealthy fathers live with their parents in expectation of inheriting the estate. Arkad did not approve of this custom. Therefore, when his son Nomasir reached adulthood, he told him that before he should succeed to his estate, he must prove that he had art capable of supporting it.

"To start thee well," he said, "I will give thee . . . a bag of gold . . . and this clay tablet upon which is carved the five laws of gold." And with that Nomasir went off to seek his fortune. After 10 years on his own, Nomasir returned to give an account of his adventures to his father.

Nomasir admitted to wasting the gold in investments he knew nothing about until all was lost and he was in adverse poverty. Just as he was about to be forced into slavery, he remembered his father's other gift -- the tablet with the five laws of gold written on it. He studied the tablet, memorized its laws, and began applying them to his daily life. In particular:

1. He began saving a tenth of his income, even though his income was small.
2. He invested that gold wisely.
3. He searched for good financial advice and got it.
4. He invested only in businesses he knew about.
5. He was not tempted by deals that were too good to be true.

By practicing the five laws of gold, Nomasir was able to get out of debt and acquire wealth. So much wealth did he acquire, in fact, that he was able to pay back his father not only the bag of gold he'd been given but three additional bags for the wisdom. This, he did to prove "how much greater value" he considered the wisdom than the gold. Nomasir had proven to his father Arkad that he could be entrusted with his estate.

And that's exactly how it works today. Until you've proven you know how to safeguard, invest, and develop wealth, few people will trust you with it. But once you have learned the secrets of wise investing, all sorts of people will want to invest their money in your projects. That is exactly what happened to billionaire Warren Buffet.

The big idea of this chapter of "The Richest Man in Babylon" -- that a good strategy for wealth building is more important than money itself -- is indisputable.

Nelson Letshwene

*"Money follows the character of its owner"*

# *35*

---

## Why Are You Stuck?

*"Man has his future within him, dynamically alive at this present moment."*
Abraham Maslow

In his book, *Influence – Science and Practice*, Robert Cialdini writes about a study carried out by a pair of Canadian psychologists (Knox & Inkster, 1968) uncovering something fascinating about people at the racetrack: just after placing bets they are much more confident of their horse's chances of winning than they were immediately before laying down the bets. Of course, nothing about the horse's chances actually shifts; it's the same horse, on the same track, in the same field; but in the minds of those bettors, its prospects improve significantly once that ticket is purchased. Although a bit puzzling at first glance, the reason for the dramatic change has to do with a common weapon of social influence that lies deep within us. It is, quite simply, our desire to be (and to appear) consistent with what we have already done. Once we make a choice or take a stand, we will encounter personal and interpersonal pressures to behave consistently with that commitment. Those pressures will cause us to respond in ways that justify our earlier decision.

**Robbie Rich:** But the same thing happens with our political parties or favourite sports clubs. Even when they're doing bad, the fact that we ever publicised that we support them, we tend to stick with them.

**Silver:** What makes that study interesting is that most of us are living exactly like that. We live a life of justification of earlier decisions. Now think about that clearly. Look at your chosen vocation. A lot of people feel 'stuck' in a career choice. Why?

**Betsy Broke:** Well you can't just go on changing your career at a whim!

**Robbie Rich:** The funny thing is that some people do change their careers, but usually very late in their lives. And they wish they had changed earlier. They didn't change because they spent more time justifying their earlier choice than seeing that it's not working.

**Betsy Broke:** Sometimes we don't change because we think, or hope, that things will get better.

**Silver:** Well think about it: what did that teenager who chose your vocation know about life?

**Betsy Broke:** What is that supposed to mean?

**Silver:** Yes, you were a teenager when you chose your vocation were you not? Now that you are in your thirties, forties or even your fifties or older, and you are working, if you find this career to be unfulfilling, why do you feel stuck in it? Why do you have to spend your entire life justifying the decisions of a teenager who knew practically nothing about life?

**Betsy Broke:** Well, maybe because it pays bills?

You see that thinking too deep will get you in trouble?

**Robbie Rich:** Is that why you came on earth, to pay bills and raise kids who will leave you in a few years?

**Silver:** The problem is that we label growth 'trouble'. If most of us did not spend our lives justifying the decisions of a teenager, we would probably grow a lot faster. This is not an argument for erratic behaviour, but this is worth thinking about. Your progress in life is of utmost importance.

**Robbie Rich:** The question is: when or why did we get stuck?

**Silver:** Consider the picture that most of us go through in our lives: As a child you looked forward to everything ahead with exuberance. Every birthday was special. Progression from the lower grades to high school was the ultimate growth. If you were fortunate enough, there was tertiary education where you grew in leaps and bounds soaking up that new information and learning problem solving skills. If you are much older you have progressed to a job and you did look forward to it. Then there was marriage and kids ... and ... career ... and ... career ... and ... are you getting stuck? Have you stopped dreaming? Around age 30 to 40, most people get stuck. Why?

**Betsy Broke:** By this age most of us are stuck because we have become disillusioned.

**Silver:** Which will take us to that all important question: What do you want in life?

**Betsy Broke:** I reckon at the end of the day we all want similar things in life ...

**Robbie Rich:** Yeah, lots of money ...

**Betsy Broke:** Not only that. We all want to be happy in life. We want fulfilment in our chosen vocation. We want companionship – meaningful relationships ... and the rest of life seems to be a process to get us there ... so this process must be enjoyable ...

**Robbie Rich:** Joie de vivre – the joy of living

**Silver:** Having spoken about setting goals previously, perhaps this picture might help to bring in the urgency, or the realisation that if you don't stop and start dreaming again, then life becomes downhill. Even all the way to the divorce court or the grave.

**Robbie Rich:** There is this question that is often asked to check your passion: "What is the one thing that you will do whether someone paid you for it or not?"

**Betsy Broke:** I think the idea that you could do a thing that no one values enough to pay for it, may mean that you are wasting time.

**Silver:** Another question is: "What is the one thing that when you do, you lose track of time?" Could that be your calling? Could that be your purpose? Is your longing your calling?

**Robbie Rich:** What would you do if you were not afraid?

**Betsy Broke:** Do I need to answer all these questions?

**Silver:** If you feel stuck, and you want to be unstuck, you cannot avoid answering these questions.

# *36*

## Your Psychology of Money

*"You playing small does not serve the world."*
Nelson Mandela

**Silver:** There are two parts to money, as there are indeed to many things in the world of relativity. The Strategy and The Psychology of Money.

**Robbie Rich:** What is the Psychology of money?

**Silver:** The best way to describe it is for us to discuss it through questions. Have you ever wondered why it is said that only 2% of lottery winners ever get to retain their wealth?

**Betsy Broke:** I don't win much in competitions. I didn't even know that only few winners actually end up rich.

**Robbie Rich:** Yes, it is truly amazing that it is said that 98% of lottery winners go broke within 2 to 10 years. Why is that?

**Silver:** Have you heard of the National Basketball Association (NBA) in the United States of America?

**Robbie Rich:** Well, yes. I watch those guys every week. They make mega bucks too.

**Silver:** It is said that by the time they retire, over 90% of them are broke. Many of them are doing menial jobs to survive, and some are homeless.

**Robbie Rich:** What would have happened to all their money?

**Silver:** To get an answer to that question we have to look at the Psychology of money. What you don't know about money will hurt you. Some people have built a faulty psychology about money.

**Betsy Broke:** That is probably why many people who win government tenders worth millions of bucks may also end up broke within a few months and abandon projects.

**Robbie Rich:** Is it because they buy fancy cars

and expensive things until the money runs out?

**Silver:** Not really. There's absolutely nothing wrong with fancy cars and expensive stuff. The really wealthy also buy fancy cars and expensive stuff.

**Betsy Broke:** So is this where the faulty Psychology of money comes in?

**Silver:** Yes and No. It is really a faulty strategy. But your strategy is born of your psychology. So if your psychology is faulty, you are likely to produce a faulty strategy.

**Robbie Rich:** You just lost me!

**Silver:** Hang in there. Have you heard of "delayed gratification"?

**Betsy Broke:** Yeah, that means you must delay your gratification until you are ready to sustain it.

**Silver:** Essentially that's true. You must follow the strategy of "Wealth before lifestyle". That is the strategy of the wealthy.

**Robbie Rich:** Yeah but that assumes that you already have money. What about a guy like me who is currently living paycheque to paycheque?

**Silver:** If you don't change your psychology you

will continue to live paycheque to paycheque for the rest of your life, even if I gave you ten million bucks right now.

**Robbie Rich:** Try me.

**Betsy Broke:** Just like lottery winners and ball players. How does that work?

**Silver:** The psychology of scarcity keeps you in scarcity. The psychology of abundance grows your wealth.

**Betsy Broke:** What is that supposed to mean?

**Silver:** The simplest way to explain this is to say that your beliefs perpetuate your life. If you believe that money is scarce, subconsciously you won't even "see" it when it is there in abundance, so you will return in reality to that which you see subconsciously. But if you believe in abundance, you will "see" money even when "it's not there".

**Robbie Rich:** How do I change my psychology?

**Silver:** Do you remember that book, *As A Man Thinketh*, by James Allen?

**Robbie Rich:** Yeah. I haven't quite had enough time to finish reading it it.

**Silver:** That is the difference between you and

the wealthy. We agreed you would read it and write feedback or some notes. The idea of writing feedback is the process that will help you to understand the book. If you have to write something down, you have to think about it. But if you are lazy to think, you will read and toss aside. You need to get involved in this process.

**Betsy Broke:** Yeah, we need to work on this psychology stuff, if it will make that much of a difference.

**Silver:** True. In the book, ***Faith and Purpose***[19] mentioned earlier, this subject is discussed in more details.

Robbie Rich: So I suppose we have to delve deeper in understanding this psychology of money thing.

Silver: Indeed we must. We will take it step by step and examine our money beliefs, that often form the foundations of our psychology of money.

---

[19] Nelson Letshwene, *Faith and Purpose – Living Your Life to the Full, Without Guilt, Fear, or Regrets,* Moedi Publishing, 2014. Also available on amazon.com

*"Educate and inform the whole mass of people. They are the only sure reliance for the preservation of our liberty"*
Thomas Jefferson

# *37*

## **Your Beliefs And Money**

*"Most people do not realise that thinking about something is inviting the essence of that "something" into their experience "*
Esther & Jerry Hicks

**Betsy Broke**: What is this thing about money and beliefs. Is it really true that my beliefs about money affect my reality?

**Silver:** You should never underestimate the power of your beliefs. Many of us believe things we don't even know we believe. Because of that, we are unable to control the things that are brought to us by our beliefs. Your beliefs affect EVERYTHING about your life.

**Betsy Broke**: How does that work?

**Silver:** Consider this: If you DESIRE more money, but you go around believing that there's not enough money around, or that money is scarce, how will that belief influence the way you act?

**Robbie Rich**: I guess I might not put as much effort into trying to get the money.

**Silver:** Let's use an example that may be easier: If you DESIRE to lose weight, but you believe that diets and exercises DO NOT WORK for you, how do you think that belief will influence your actions? Will you go on a diet?

**Betsy Broke**: No, you already believe it won't work!

**Silver:** Will you go to the gym?

**Robbie Rich**: No, you already believe that it won't work.

**Silver**: What will you do?

**Robbie Rich:** Nothing other than what you've already been doing. You will continue to get fat. Your belief will override your desire.

**Silver:** Back to our money example: If you DESIRE more money, but you believe that money is scarce, how will that belief influence your actions?

**Robbie Rich**: This belief breeds cutthroat competitions and the survival of the fittest mentality. This belief gets others to be corrupt and do whatever it takes to get to the money first, before someone else does.

**Betsy Broke**: This belief gets others to cheat, steal, and get in trouble. I guess just the idea that there's not enough is scary for most of us. Such a belief is not healthy!

**Silver:** What if you believed differently? What if you believed that there's enough for everyone, and that your opportunity is just around the corner?

**Betsy Broke**: I guess you'd feel less threatened, and more committed to deliver your service or product so that you can get your share. I guess you might also be more generous and more sharing, knowing that there's enough for everyone.

**Robbie Rich**: But for most of us, our reality is that there is not enough. You can't just come here and start telling me that if I believed that there's plenty, then there'll be plenty.

**Silver:** The reality of an overweight person is that diets and exercises do not work. But the reality of a healthy lean person is that diets and exercises work. You create your own reality.

**Robbie Rich**: Wait a minute. I think I need more clarification on this subject.

**Silver:** Now you are starting to open up your mind. Read an essay called *The Desire for Prosperity*. It's part of a book called **Your Longing is Your Calling – The seven desires of life** [20]

**Betsy Broke**: The idea that if you desire to lose excess weight, you can't go around believing that no diet ever works for you intrigues me.

**Silver**: Your belief will override your desire. You will act out your belief. That is what we always do. We act out our beliefs. Our beliefs are stronger than our desires. If you desire good health, you can't go around believing that there is

---

[20] R Nelson Letshwene, 2015, Your Longing Is Your Calling, Moedi Publishing. Also abailable on amazon.com

no cure for your ailment. Your belief overrides your desire. You'll lose hope and stop looking for a cure.

**Betsy Broke:** So, can we tie back that idea that most lottery winners end up broke? Did they not believe that they could win?

**Silver:** Good point. They believed they could win. But many of them have never believed they could be wealthy. So they have no beliefs that sustain wealth.

**Robbie Rich:** So, when they get money, with their scarcity mentality, they believe they need to spend it before it runs out?

**Silver:** And that's how they run out of it. They are afraid because it might run out, and so it does.

**Robbie Rich:** Wait, what if they got counselling and they get shown strategies to retain their wealth?

**Silver:** Pride often gets in the way. And as you know, pride comes before the fall. Besides, building a belief system is not a function of just one lecture or one counselling session. For most people, as soon as they know they have the money, they have already spent it in their minds before they even lay hands on it. The financial advisor may be speaking to the wind.

**Betsy Broke:** So then, it's better to build a positive psychology of money even long before I come into huge money?

**Silver:** Yes. That's why positive affirmations on a daily basis are important even when you don't have the money. That foundation will preserve your money, however little that comes in, until it builds up.

# 38

# Wherever You Go, There You Will Be

*"Include yourself among those you love."*
Neale Donald Walsch

**Robbie Rich:** You mentioned the strategy of "Wealth before lifestyle". What exactly is that?
**Silver:** It fits in with the strategy of "Delayed gratification", in fact, it may be the same thing. It's got to do with creating what is called a financial pipe-line. That means you must have a system that will keep bringing money into your life so that no matter how much you spend, the money does not stop pouring in. You focus on building your wealth, before you focus on your lifestyle.

Extravagant lifestyle does not support your wealth, but if you build your wealth first, then you can have an extravagant lifestyle.

**Betsy Broke:** It sounds like we are now talking about strategy. Let's get back to the psychology of money. How do I change my psychology?

**Silver:** Let me tell you a parable, as told by Deepak Chopra, author of *Creating Affluence*.

A woman left her village in search of a new village to relocate to. When she finally got to some new village that she thought she would like, she decided to go and ask the wisest elder of the village what kind of people lived there.

The wise village elder said to her: 'before I tell you the kinds of people who live in this village, tell me the kinds of people who lived in the village you came from'.

The woman said: 'you wouldn't believe how terrible those people are. They gossip, they steal, they are untrustworthy, and they are always trying to pull you down. It is impossible to make progress in that village, that is why I decided it is time to move'.

The wise man looked at the woman sadly and said, 'I'm afraid that this village has exactly the same kinds of people. There is no difference between where you came from and here. I suggest you just settle back at your village, at least it will save you the cost of moving, but of course you can move here if you want. Welcome home.'

Disappointed, the woman stormed out and left.

Immediately after she left, came another woman to the wise man who was also looking to relocate to the village and came to ask the wise man of the village the same question.

In like manner the wise man asked the woman to describe the kinds of people where she came from.

The new woman said: 'I would really hate to leave my people. They are the kindest people on the universe. The village I came from is filled with opportunities galore. People are serving and loving each other. I would actually be sad to leave my village unless I can find a similar village'.

The wise man smiled and said to the woman, this village will be an excellent home for you. There is no difference between where you came from and here. If you choose to stay, you will feel just at home. Welcome home.'

**Betsy Broke:** Wait a minute, I thought this wise man just told the other woman that the village was as rotten as her old village, why is he now saying the village is full of angels?

**Silver:** What the old wise man meant was that your world always exists within you. Wherever you go, there you will be. Your psychology is your view of the world around you.

**Betsy Broke:** So the woman who believes in troublesome people always experiences trouble, while the one who believes in the goodness of people tends to experience more of that? Isn't that just psychobabble?

**Robbie Rich:** So the one with the psychology of scarcity will eventually experience scarcity, even though they have ten million bucks? Doesn't that mean we are doomed?

**Silver:** No, you are not doomed. You can change your psychology. That is why Dr. Wayne Dyer says: "*change the way you look at things, and the things you look at change*". There is an essay that illustrates this clearly called: *The Sermon That Caused The Preacher's Fall*[21].

---

[21] Nelson Letshwene, *The Sermon That Caused The Preacher's Fall. Available from* www.amazon.com *in paperback and kindle.*

*"There are two sources of unhappiness in life. One is not getting what you want; the other is getting it."*
George Bernard Shaw

# 39

## You Are Your Wealth.

*"It is only with the heart that one can see rightly; what is essential is invisible to the eye"*
Antoine de Saint-Exupéry

**Robbie Rich:** People say you come into the world with nothing and you leave with nothing. So trying to gather wealth is a waste of time.

**Betsy Broke:** That is depressing. It actually makes life pointless doesn't it?

**Silver:** Well, I don't agree with those people. I think you come into the world with little, and you go out with a whole lot more than you brought in.

**Robbie Rich:** How's that?

**Silver:** As Mark Victor Hansen and Robert Allen point out in their book, *The One Minute*

*Millionaire*, the problem with the traditional balance sheet is that it leaves out a lot more than it includes. It only includes your tangible assets and liabilities. But it does not acknowledge that those tangible assets would not have been there in the first place, had it not been for your intangible assets.

**Betsy Broke:** But if you don't have money you can't do anything.

**Silver:** Perhaps. But even that is partly incorrect. If you don't have an idea, you can't do anything. Now, what price can you place on an idea?

**Robbie Rich:** Oh, I think I like this. You mean we should have an internal balance sheet.

**Silver:** Absolutely. Let's construct one. What assets would you put on your internal balance sheet?

**Robbie Rich:** Creativity, Imagination, Courage, persistence, valuable skills like selling, persuasion, management, contacts, and relationships.

**Silver:** Good. Can you see how all these internal assets can help you in your wealth building, and yet none of them appear as assets on your traditional balance sheet? Now, can you figure out what would be your internal liabilities, things that would work against you?

**Betsy Broke:** Fear, small mindedness, negativity, procrastination, laziness, poor organisation, anger, self-pity, and pettiness.

**Silver:** Again, can you see how these internal liabilities will hold you back, and yet they can't be measured financially?

**Robbie Rich:** Oh I see, so a person with an internal negative net worth will always end up with an external negative net worth. Is that what you meant by saying 'your psychology determines your strategy'?

**Silver:** Exactly. A person whose dominant character is small mindedness, or laziness, or any of the internal liabilities, even if you gave them ten million bucks, they cannot create the vision to grow the money. So in the end, they remain poor.

**Betsy Broke:** That is why a person whose dominant character is creativity, visionary, imagination, or courage can start with nothing and keep growing their net worth?

**Silver:** Correct. All you really need to get started is three things: a good idea; the commitment to carry it out; and the key contacts that posses all other resources, because in the end, you are your wealth.

**Betsy Broke:** So why do you believe that when you die you go out with a whole lot more than you brought in?

**Silver:** Just imagine: if you could inherit your parents' experience, wisdom, and courage, wouldn't you be better off than inheriting the symbols of their wealth?

**Betsy Broke:** But people say those things are valueless simply because you cannot will them to your offspring.

**Silver:** Well, that goes back to your definition of your purpose in life. Do you consider valuable only things that will be considered valuable by others, that is, things that can appear on other people's balance sheets, or things that make your life here worth living?

**Robbie Rich:** Now I see why working on my psychology, – my internal balance sheet – is very important. It will determine what I do with whatever money I get.

**Betsy Broke:** So you come into the world with such assets as your natural talents, and by your experiences on earth, you go out with more.

**Silver:** Your internal balance sheet is what you go out with. At funerals, people often recount your internal balance sheet.

**Betsy Broke:** You have persuaded me to think differently about my psychology of money.

**Robby Rich:** It is a topic that requires an entire book.

"Eternal vigilance is the price of liberty"

# *40*

---

## The Voice From Within

*"Those who are afraid to fail are essentially afraid to succeed because they'll never try anything new"*
Todd Duncan

**Silver:** Have you ever had a brilliant idea, and before you could do anything with it, you see someone else doing exactly the same business that you thought of before, except you know you never told anybody about it?

**Robbie Rich:** Yes, it has happened to me many times.

**Silver:** What stopped you from following through with your idea?

**Betsy Broke:** Self-doubt. There's this little voice that keeps telling you that this won't work. But how come somebody else is making the same business work?

**Robbie Rich:** I guess it's back to the internal balance sheet. My internal liabilities are greater than my internal assets?

**Silver:** That could be so. Those who succeed are those with an internal voice that encourages them all the time. It never criticises them, but it always encourages. It's the voice that says:

You can do it!

Go for it!

You did it – Hurray!

Good for you!

You are awesome!

Give it another try!

Do you have a voice like that internally?

**Betsy Broke:** Oh no. All mine says is:

Who do you think you are?

You can't do that!

What an idiot!

You don't have enough education to attempt that!

Where have you ever seen that?

You'll probably fail anyway!

You're so clumsy!

**Robbie Rich:** Yeah. I'm starting to see that there is more going on inside of me than I thought before. I always thought my problems were the circumstances outside of me over which I have no control.

**Silver:** Well, you need to start with yourself. The rich and the poor operate within the same circumstances. Listen to yourself. Which voice is the loudest? Is it the voice of encouragement or the voice of discouragement? Is it a voice that highlights your weaknesses or a voice that lifts your strengths and seeks to make you stronger?

**Betsy Broke:** But what's this got to do with making more money?

**Silver:** Well, we said money is an idea. If your ideas can never get off the ground because of your negative voice, you'll never make the money you wish to make.

**Robbie Rich:** How do I overcome my negative voice?

**Silver:** Notice your internal dialogue. Stop criticising yourself. Learn to praise yourself.

**Betsy Broke:** Isn't it wrong to blow your own trumpet?

**Silver:** Remember you are not trying to convince anybody but yourself. This is first of all, private work. This is the voice from within. In any case, how come you are comfortable criticising yourself in public but uncomfortable praising yourself in public? There's something wrong with a society that delights in your weaknesses and gets embarrassed at your strengths. Write down positive affirmations and repeat them to yourself everyday until you believe them.

I can do it.

I am worthy.

I am good enough.

I am competent.

I'm smart enough to figure this out.

I can afford it if I really want it.

# 41

---

# Where Is The Cash Cow

*"If only God would give me one clear sign! Like making a deposit in my name in a Swiss bank account"*

Woody Allen

One of the things you will have to do and do it quickly even as you are continuing to set the foundation of your life, is find the cash cow.

**Betsy Broke:** What is the cash cow?

**Silver:** The cash cow is an income producing system that you have set up in place. You have your primary cash cow, and as soon as possible, you need to set up your next cash cow, and many others after that.

**Robbie Rich:** Until you have a kraal full of them

...

**Betsy Broke:** But all I have now is my job. Would that be my primary cash cow?

**Silver:** Yes, unless it's not. And like a real cow, you need to take care of it, and don't just dump it before you establish other systems out there.

**Robbie Rich:** So the primary cash cow should provide me with enough milk to feed myself, an also give me some to sell?

**Silver:** As a matter of speaking, yes.

**Betsy Broke:** I feel like my job is jus there to maintain the status quo. How do I break free from that and start growing new streams of income?

**Silver:** You need to start thinking of multiple streams of income. But don't kill your current cash cow before your next one is ready to feed you.

**Robbie Rich:** What when the current cash cow gets old and is not producing what it used to produce before? In terms of quantity of milk and satisfaction levels.

**Silver:** You may want to read that book by Spencer Johnson, *Who moved my cheese?*

Cheese is a metaphor for the things we like such as work and relationships. He says cheese does get old. Change is the only thing that's constant. Be ready to move before your cheese gets stale.

Now, what you feed yourself will determine whether you get strong or you get weak. As we have said here before, feed your mind. Don't go lifestyle before wealth building. Invest in your financial and personal education.

**Betsy Broke:** So this refers to the books I read and the people I spend time with.

**Silver:** Yes. Gather your team together, your mentors, and coaches. Spend time with people who are already playing a bigger better game than you are. As one wise man said, five years from now, you are exactly the same person you are today except for the books you read and the people you spend time with.

**Robbie Rich:** What are the other cash cows?

**Silver:** We have already discussed them here in different forms, but they largely remain hidden to a person with a faulty internal dialogue, because perception always comes from within, and it creates your experience. That is why it is called in-sight.

**Robbie Rich:** Does that mean as long as the negative voice is louder than the positive voice, I will never see opportunities even if they were in front of me?

**Silver:** You will recall that we have spoken about having a dream. From that dream, comes your SMART goals. Your goals could include any of the cash cows we have already discussed.

They include real estate investments, businesses such as network marketing that have low start up costs, and of course other businesses based on your passion, skills and talents.

**Betsy Broke:** How do you milk such cash cows?

**Silver:** Acquire them first, one by one. Some, such as those based on skills and talents may need to be developed. Make a decision that each day, you will do at least one activity that will propel you forward. First reinforce your commitments: getting out of debt if you're still in it. Commit to savings, investing, and to learning and growing. That may mean read one good book per month or set an annual target for the books you need to read. Then move on to such activities as marketing; for example, one phone call a day to one new client, especially if you are in network marketing, or any business for that matter.

**Robbie Rich:** What if your interest is real estate?

**Silver:** Remember that real estate is a capital-intensive business. Mix that up with ideas that need less cash but could produce an income. But if real estate is your chosen thing, then make a decision to analyse say one property per week or per month, or whatever time period works for you. You are not buying, you are just analysing. Look at the figures and see what they tell you. Get property analysis software or use a spread sheet. Focus on income producing activities.

**Betsy Broke:** Or explore new business ideas and see if you can't get one that flows with you.

**Robbie Rich:** Or check out the Internet and see if you can't utilise it to grow your business idea, or run a 24/7 business on the Internet.

**Betsy Broke:** Or research and write a book on

your favourite subject …

**Silver:** Make it your ambition to find that cash cow …

# *42*

---

# The Good Samaritan Wasn't Broke – The Generous Spirit

*""Come to the edge", he said. "We are afraid", they said. "Come to the edge", he said. They came, He pushed them, and they flew"*
Apollinaire.

**Robbie Rich:** The psychology of a lot of people about money is the belief that having too much money means you are greedy. Many people would like to have money but they are also afraid of becoming heartless.

**Silver:** I don't know who you are hanging out with, but money, like a weapon, is neither good nor bad. It is those who wield it who can be thus categorised.

**Betsy Broke:** Yes, people would rather just be the Good Samaritans and help others.

**Silver:** Have you considered the fact that the Good Samaritan[22] was not broke? There is not a single helper or giver who has nothing to give. Therefore, to get, you must also be willing to give.

**Betsy Broke:** How can I give what I do not have?

**Silver:** Back to your view of the world again. Do you really believe that you came into this world with absolutely nothing; therefore the world owes you everything without you giving anything in return?

**Robbie Rich:** That is very interesting. Does that mean you need to focus on being a giver, and you will get?

**Betsy Broke:** You can't give what you do not have!

**Silver:** Indeed that is true. You cannot give what you perceive to be missing from your life. Consider this: The law of reciprocity, otherwise

---

[22] Luke 10:30-37

know as the Golden Rule states that whatsoever you do for others, you have done unto God, and of course unto yourself. Or more directly, do to others as you would have them do unto you. What can you give? You give what you have. You have talents. Give your time, your approval, your smile, your advice, your wisdom, your compliments, your love. All these things will flow back to you in abundance. Remember the law of the farm?

**Betsy Broke:** Which one is that?

**Silver:** You reap what you sow. If you want to reap a harvest of wealth and abundance, well, now is your chance to start sowing seeds of giving. You get what you give. The one who gives the most love receives the most love from people. The one who gives the most criticisms, receives more criticisms from people. If you want people to love you, you must love them, but you must not do it with a view to receiving from them anything. You must trust that the power of the universe will give back to you.

**Betsy Broke:** Yeah, but some friends are selfish.

They only come to you to see what they can get, and then they leave.

**Silver:** If that is your view of the world, then that is the kind of friends you will always attract. Think about it. What did the Good Samaritan give?

**Robbie Rich:** He gave a lot. He even paid for a stranger to stay in an hotel.

**Silver:** Consider another thought, there is hardly a hero in the Bible who was broke.

**Robbie Rich:** Is that why it is said it is more blessed to give than to receive? Your blessing will come from above?

# *43*

---

# Other People's Resources

*"A single conversation across the table with a wise
man is worth a month's study of books."*
A Chinese Proverb.

**Robbie Rich:** I think everyone knows that it is difficult to pull anything off by yourself. Becoming rich must be a team effort.

**Silver:** Absolutely. To get rich you need a whole lot more resources than any one man can amass by himself. You need to find a way to use other people's resources.

**Betsy Broke:** There are too many people abusing others for success. There is something seriously faulty with that system.

**Silver:** Yes, abusing people will never get you

anywhere. That is why you need your own team, bound together by the same mission.

**Robbie Rich:** What are the resources that I will need before I know what kind of a team to gather together?

**Silver:** Good question. Mark Victor Hansen and Robert Allen discuss resources in their book, *The One Minute Millionaire* that we mentioned earlier. The first resource to think about is of course money. Depending on what your chosen field of investment is, you need an investor into your idea. In real estate investing, you buy residential real estate by only putting down 10%, and your partner, the bank, puts down the rest, but you control the whole 100%. This is a resource called Other People's money. (OPM)

**Robbie Rich:** What are the other resources?

**Silver:** Other People's Experience, (OPE). The quickest way to gain other people's experience is to apprentice yourself with someone who's made it. Get a mentor. Learn all they know, meet all their contacts, and do what they do. If this is not possible, then read their books; listen to their audio programs; watch their videos; attend their seminars, take their home-study programs. This opens the scope up to a lot of people that you can choose from. Leverage is about maximising your results in a minimum amount of time.

**Robbie Rich:** I guess the next thing is Other People's Ideas, (OPI)?

**Silver:** That's correct. You only need to make sure that you are not stealing patented ideas. You get your own ideas from listening to other people talk about their own ideas. When you read books, attend seminars, and watch videos, your mind starts working to create ideas for yourself, but you would not have come up with those ideas on your own, had your mind not been stimulated.

**Betsy Broke:** This all sounds great, but unfortunately it takes a lot of time to gather all this. Someone like me stuck in a full time job can never do this.

**Silver:** Which is why the next thing to use is Other People's Time (OPT). People can sell you their time, talent, connections, resources and know-how relatively inexpensively. For example if you are in direct marketing, you can buy lists off of the Internet and start marketing directly. Someone else put their time into gathering the list, you just buy it. If you have a great book idea but have not the time to do the research, you can get a ghost-writer. She will do the necessary research, and put the book together for you.

Finally, you can use Other People's Work (OPW). Most people want a job. They want security rather than opportunity. Hire and delegate all that you can't do.

Leverage yourself through other people's resources and grow.

# 44

---

# What's In A Hire-Purchase Contract?

"Buyer Beware" is an important saying in consumer law, which means a buyer must always be careful when buying something to ensure that there is nothing wrong with it. This alerts consumers to be vigilant and to always learn to read between the lines. Ever heard the saying, "if something sounds too good to true, it often is"?

Hire purchase (HP), now known as Instalment Sale Agreement, is a form of credit. It is a way to buy goods when you cannot afford to pay the full amount straight away. It is often used to buy household appliances, furniture, clothing and cars.

While cash is king and you are better off buying cash, not everyone is able to accumulate the whole amount to buy things for cash when they need them. So they opt to take it now and pay later or pay as you go.

You therefore need to educate yourself and be aware of what a hire-purchase agreement implies to you. Don't sign that contract until you know what you are signing for.

You need to be aware that while most advertisers will display a lower cash price, often indicating how much you are saving if you buy the goods now, such savings do not get passed on to those who buy on credit.

In most cases you pay more than the price on the price tag. Hire purchase includes interest and other administrative costs.

Compare the rates and other costs at several shops before you buy. Remember that the interest rate AND the other costs affect the total cost of hire purchase. Find out if a bank loan would be cheaper than hire purchase finance.

When you buy goods on hire purchase, you and

the seller sign a written agreement, which must contain information about how many payments you will be making, how often to pay (e.g. weekly, monthly), the amount to pay, when to pay, where to pay and the name and address of the seller.

You should never sign this agreement in a hurry without understanding what you are signing for. Don't sign for someone else either, otherwise you may be signing surety unaware.

Who qualifies for instalment sale agreement? Generally, retailers will not enter into a hire purchase deal with you if your credit history is poor, meaning you have a habit of not paying your debt or paying too late. Ironically, if you have never had credit, you might fall in the same category as having a poor credit history and therefore may be denied credit. If they can't determine your credit character, they are likely to say no. Your credit character is determined, not only by your salary and other debts that you have and how you are dealing with them. Questions they ask on the form help them to make some decision even before they go to the credit bureaux. A question like how long you've been at your current address, and the one before, helps them to see whether or not you are in the habit of moving, which may be difficult for them to track you in the future, or not.

Now to the big question: what is the cost of a hire-purchase contract? To get the **amount financed** the seller adds the following figures together: the cash price of the goods (not the reduced cash price – that one is for those who buy cash, but the full price); freight/delivery charges, (Oh yes, nothing is for free); installation charges (if necessary); statutory fees (e.g., cost of motor vehicle registration if buying a car on hire purchase); legal costs for drafting the contract; repayment or credit life insurance, which has been made compulsory by most sellers; other charges (e.g., the cost of extra accessories for the goods), and this gives the total price (not the total debt).

THEN DEDUCT FROM THAT TOTAL: your deposit, and/or the value of any trade-in you offer. The Total cost of credit is determined by

ADDING interest (or 'Finance Charge'), booking fee, maintenance and repairs, property insurance required by sellers as well as other charges (e.g., a fee to check your credit rating from the credit bureaux). This is the additional cost of the transaction over the cash transaction.

Adding the **AMOUNT FINANCED** and **TOTAL COST** of credit together will give you the amount you have to pay back. This is called the **Balance payable** on the hire purchase agreement. Of course a simple addition of your instalments plus your deposit will reveal that you are paying a whole lot more than the advertised price.

You have to remember that with instalment sale agreements, the goods are not yours until you pay the last penny, and if you fail to pay, they can come and reposses them up, but that does not release you from the debt. There are however procedures that the seller needs to follow before they pick up the goods, like giving you a warning and a chance to rescue yourself, after which they can get a court order to repossess and pick up the goods from you and revalue them, to determine you remaining debt.

Always get a copy of your agreement and go through it. Make sure you get a receipt every time you pay, and keep them safe. If you are paying by debit order through the bank, keep your bank statements as your receipts. Expect a statement every month from the seller, showing what you have paid and what you owe. Remember that the quicker you pay off the goods, the lower the amount of extra charges you will pay.

# *45*

---

# Who Is On Your TEAM?

*"Give me a lever long enough, and a prop strong enough and I will single handedly move the world."*
Archimedes (c. 287 – 212 b.c.)

**Silver:** According to Mark Victor Hansen and Robert Allen who co-authored *The One Minute Millionaire*, there are six key forms of leverage that give you maximum impact.

**Betsy Broke:** What is leverage?

**Silver:** Leverage is the power to control a lot with just a little.

**Betsy Broke:** Like using other people's resources?

**Robbie Rich:** Absolutely. Now the trick is, how

do you get those people to you so that you can use their resources?

**Silver:** Consider the six forms of leverage spoken of by Hansen and Allen in their book. They are: Mentors, Teams, Networks, Infinite Networks, Tools and skills, and Systems. If you apply all of these forms of leverage to a pure smart goal, you are unstoppable.

**Robbie Rich:** Those sound interesting. How does this model work?

**Silver:** If you work alone, you are without leverage. You have to rely on your own knowledge, your own experience, your own money, and your own resources. Most of those who quit because of fatigue and discouragement are those who attempt to go at it alone.

**Robbie Rich:** That is why mentors are so important, because they know what to do.

**Silver:** But also, most importantly, they know what NOT to do.

**Betsy Broke:** Does your team have to consist of experienced business people? Most business people don't have time for inexperienced learners.

**Silver:** Which is a pity, but fortunately your team does not have to consist of experienced business people. But it would help if your mentor or coach is experienced. Your team just has to be people with a common purpose. You will be surprised the vast amount of knowledge and experience that exists when a team of any kind gets together. One knows something about the Internet; one something about marketing; one has incredible people skills, etc.

**Betsy Broke:** Oh that's a relief. You mean I can just gather my friends who want to change their lives together and we start brainstorming?

**Silver:** Yes and no. Not all of your friends would qualify. You are where you are because of the people you've been hanging with. So choosing new circle of influence is also part of the deal. Some people you will have to deliberately exclude.

**Robbie Rich:** That's an interesting point but true. Some people are too toxic to hang around.

**Silver:** Even if you have not yet identified a

mentor, one of you might know someone who might be interested in mentoring or coaching the group.

**Betsy Broke:** That's great, you mean we just get together and start talking?

**Silver:** That is how great ideas are formed and many great success stories come from people just getting together to talk. Of course you are deliberately talking about how to change your lives, not just about gossip. A brainstorming session would be a great place to start.

**Robbie Rich:** What about the other four forms of leverage, how do you build them?

**Silver:** Let's focus on those next time.

# *46*

## **Accidental Mentors**

*"If you can tell me who your heroes are, I can tell you how you're going to turn out in life."*
Warren Buffett

**Betsy Broke:** What if your team finds it difficult to recruit a mentor? What do you do then?

**Silver:** Maybe we should define the different types of mentoring opportunities that are available out there. While it may be ideal to get someone who is experience who is willing to put time aside to help your group, those chances are very slim since everybody is so busy with their own stuff. So there exists at least three types of mentoring opportunities.

**Betsy Broke:** I thought there was only the

hands-on mentor. The one who needs to put aside time to teach me and the group what to do.

**Silver:** Actually, a hands-on mentor is not even someone who will teach you class-room style, they are almost always on the run. The way you get them to teach you is you find a way to attach yourself to them, while they are going about their own business.

**Robbie Rich:** So hands-on is really on-the-run? It seems I will have to 'work' for this person for a while?

**Silver:** As Robert Kiyosaki says: don't take a job for what you can earn, but take a job for what you can learn.

**Betsy Broke:** Too late for me. I've got bills to pay.

**Silver:** You keep that attitude you will be paying bills for the rest of your life.

**Robbie Rich:** What other mentoring opportunities are out there?

**Silver:** You have what is called the 'accidental mentor'. There are many of those and fortunately they are everywhere!

**Robbie Rich:** Are those the ones you meet by accident?

**Silver:** In a way yes. If you are open and teachable, each person you meet can "accidentally" teach you something to advance your cause. If you keep the attitude that "nothing happens by accident", then every event or occurrence, no matter how trivial, has a potential for "accidental mentorship".

**Betsy Broke:** Oh, that means I can learn something from everyone I meet!

**Silver:** True, but not just everyone, but everything. The accidental mentor does not have to be a person. It's anything that causes you to change the course of your life or to advance your cause.

**Robbie Rich:** Like reading a powerful book.

**Silver:** Especially powerful books. When Warren Buffet, touted to be the best investor in the world today, was in college, he read a book by Benjamin Graham called *The Intelligent Investor* that changed his life. Not only did he seek out this author, he enrolled in his class and got a master's degree in economics. Then after graduation he persisted and worked for the Graham Investment company, (he even offered to work for free). After two years, Buffet launched himself, investing a whopping $100! Today, we only know him as a billionaire

# *47*

# Success Without A Vote – A Short History Of How We Got Here

*"If Columbus had an advisory committee he would probably still be at the dock."*

Arthur J. Goldberg

When major technological breakthroughs take over the world, most of the world's populations do not get to vote. You did not vote for the Internet to be a major deal in life today, yet it affects your life. You did not vote, at least not in the traditional way, to have social media change the way we communicate.

When the world shifted from the Industrial Age to

the Information age, to the Fourth Industrial Revolution, your vote was not sought. The world is changing faster than many people realise.

Consider the changeover from the Agrarian age where agricultural land was the most important commodity, and the so-called nobles who owned land controlled everything. Those who did not own land had very little chance of owning anything; they were serfs and peasants who worked the land for the rich.

The Industrial age changed all that. Since non-agricultural land was cheap, the industrialists like Harrison Ford bought lots of that cheap land and build a motor factory on that. Other industrialists followed and bought non-agricultural land to a point where this type of land became more important and thus more expensive than agricultural land. The tide was changing and soon the world became industrialised, as we know it today. Rocky land was more important than fertile agricultural land because it could hold tall skyscrapers and huge factories, and it was discovered that such land often contained other rich minerals such as iron, oil and copper that fuelled the Industrial Age.

Value was no longer placed on the land, but on the real estate improvements that were built on it like factories, warehouses, mines, and residential homes for the workers. Wealth moved from the farmers to the factory owners who sold products from the factories.

Another shift within the industrial age happened when the richer people realised the value of real estate and they started building more buildings than they themselves needed, and they rent these out to producers. Wealth was again shifting from the hardworking worker to the owners of the buildings within which they worked as rentals went up.

Many historians contend that in 1989 when the Berlin wall came down and the world wide web went up, we were officially moving from the industrial age to the Information Age.

Robert Kiyosaki in his book, *Rich Dad's Guide to Investing*, contends that it was during the Industrial Age that the 'go to school so you can find a job' idea became popular. In the Agrarian Age, a formal education was not necessary because professions were handed down from parent to child: bakers taught their children to be bakers, farmers taught their children to be farmers, etc. Near the end of this era, the idea of "a" job, or one job for life, became popularised. You went to school, got that one job for life, such as a teacher, or a nurse, you worked your way up the corporate ladder, and when you retired, the company and the government took care of you.

The Industrial Age, similar to the Agrarian age, was labour intensive. To build wealth, it took great effort and coordination as well as lots of money, people, land and power to build and control the wealth.

The Information Age has changed not all but a lot of that. Money is an idea. Entrepreneurs who cry and complain about lack of money are those who are stuck in the Industrial age. Today it is possible for individuals who financially obscure one day to be extremely rich the next day. Take a look at the pages of Fortune

Magazine and see the under forty 'kids' who are today multi-millionaires.

The fourth industrial revolution is revolutionising the way we look at life.

For the first time in world history, no longer does it take money to make money. No longer does it take vast tracks of land or resources to become rich. No longer does it take friends in high places to make money. The founders of Yahoo started in a garage. It doesn't matter what university you went to, (or dropped out from – ) or what sex, race or religion you are a part of. Money is an idea. For some people, however, the hardest thing to change is an old idea.

We see it happening today. We send kids abroad to study, and when they come back, they are looking for a job. When they don't find one, they stay home and blame the government. You need to keep track of the changes that are taking place. Look at pensions as a sign. No longer do companies pay pensions to the retirees. It is retirement annuities, to which the worker contributed during their working years that will take care of your older self. Such annuities are independent of the employer and the worker needs to keep it running even when they change jobs. Unfortunately, old ideas die hard. When people change jobs, they often spend the gratuity they receive, and there is nothing in their retirement funds, because they are stuck with the ideas of the industrial age.

Today, information is the most important thing. Stay informed about who needs what service and provide it. Sniff out the needs. Be well informed. Some people have never read a book since they left school. If that is your attitude that your degree or education is enough, you will be left behind. Even with a degree in hand, without Continuous Professional Development (CPD), you get left behind. Today we are free agents and can have many professions in our lives. No longer one job for life.

To live in the information age and then try in the midst of that to figure out what the fourth industrial revolution is all about is scary for a lot of people. Now, information should not be confused with education. There are many educated people without the "correct" kind of information. This is proven by the many unemployed graduates in cities all over the world. This is not to discount school education, which is of immense importance in some circles.

As Mark Victor Hansen[23] points out, "in the age of inexpensive computers, wireless handheld devices and ever-present low cost connections to a global communications network, workers can now own the means of production".

You must own and know how to use the tools of production – computers, programming, software, and the modern technology for you to succeed. Your team, your mentors, and your mastermind groups are all exponentially strengthened when you own these information tools and you have the skills to use them.

The world changed and you change. You have to learn how to drive a car and to play, if not to burn, a CD. No vote. Just change. You have to be

---

[23] Mark Victor Hansen: *The One Minute Millionaire*

comfortable with a computer. You have to master the use of all technologies available.

You have to get comfortable with the use of social media platforms. Traditional roles are changing ... you don't vote on these, it is called change.

Change is irresistible. As a wise man said, there is nothing as powerful as an idea whose time has come.

All what this means is that you should get in control of your destiny. You can't blame anybody now. The ball is in your court. You need to get "streetwise" and learn the systems that can help you to succeed. The good news is that only you know what you are worth, (which can be scary if you know you are being overpaid). The truth will come out because accountability systems are getting clearer and clearer, and being able to deliver can now be measured. If you were under-appreciated (which most people feel), you should rejoice because now you can show your true worth.

You can't vote on change, it just happens. (Okay

you may still be able to vote for your local councillor or Member of Parliament in a constituency based system, but that's about it ...) ... Success without a vote, because change happens, without your vote...

****

## Reader Comments

*Good day, I'm a regular reader of Silver Line column as I have realised that you do give valuable advise. I do need your help, I have been burning with this desire to start my own business but I don't know where to start. I sometimes abandon good ideas simply because I tell myself that I can't make it financially but this time I'm determine to go with this ambition. The little that I know is that I need a good business plan, market, and a supplier, to get capital from the lending institutions. What is your advice, what must be my starting point? DPT.*

# *48*

---

## What's a Business System?

*"No one knows enough to be a pessimist".*
Wayne dyer.

**Betsy Broke:** When a calendar year comes to an end I can't help but think, will I be doing the same thing next year that I did this year?

**Silver:** Well, if you did the same thing the following year as you did the year before, but you changed your attitude and the way you look at it, it could actually feel like a new thing, and you might actually enjoy it more, and experience more growth. The rule is, you must love what you do and do what you love, otherwise it will soon be a burden, it doesn't matter how much potential profits there is in an opportunity, it has to flow with you.

**Betsy Broke:** But is there an easier business to start, that is, if it flows with me?

**Robbie Rich:** Sometimes you will never know whether it flows with you or not until you do it.

**Silver:** That is correct. So, when you want to look at a business to start, you must always consider the system that makes it work.

**Robbie Rich:** What do you mean by the system?

**Silver:** Well, people often look at the product and the potential profit, but fail to find the system. Without the system, you have no business. You may have the greatest product in the market, but if you don't have a business system, you will surely fail. Let me give you an example of two systems: the Franchise system and the Network Marketing system.

**Betsy Broke:** Franchises are expensive!

**Silver:** Its relative. That may rule them out for many people, but they generally have a great system. If you can follow direction and do as you are directed, you could do well if the market is right. On the other hand, Network Marketing is another system that most people can afford. I suggest that if you don't have any business background and are serious about starting your own business, you should find a network marketing company and study its systems.

**Robbie Rich:** How exactly does a network marketing system work:

**Silver:** It is a marketing system in which individual business owners, supported by the mother company with products and often with training, recruit, train, and develop a team of product users who also become sellers and distributors of company products to others. The best ones have excellent systems that develop your personal skills, teach you about the product, and give you selling and distribution skills that you will need to be a successful business owner. These skills are essential for success in any business, and that is why I think you should start there to learn about business systems. You might actually succeed there and never have to start your own business system. It is a whole lot harder to start your own system, and without a system, success is harder.

**Robbie Rich:** What more can you tell us about Network Marketing, it seems I can learn a lot through this system?

**Silver:** Success is a personal thing. Let's look further into that system next.

# *49*

---

# Networking vs. Selling

*"Regardless of where you live, you are in the geographical centre of the world. You can go from where you are to anywhere you want to go."*

--Zig Ziglar

The principle of duplication lies at the heart of a network marketing system. A network marketing system takes into account the value of each client over a lifetime, whereas in traditional sales, a customer's value is not instantly and automatically recognised.

**Robbie Rich:** What would be the difference then between a commercial sales person and a network marketer?

**Silver:** Let's say a professional sales person, in

her normal line of work might be able to see say sixteen prospects per day, with only one in four (25%) conversion rate. Unless that sales person is tenacious and will service those clients over time and sell them more products from the company, they might never meet again. Contrast that with a network marketer who sees only half, say eight clients in a month, not a day, with only the same conversion rate of 25%, i.e. two join the network. If those two also go and see eight people with the same conversion rate, there will be six people in the network, and if those six do the same thing, then there will be 18 entrepreneurs and then 54 and so on …

**Robbie Rich:** It seems like there is a multiplication process.

**Silver:** Yes, it's exponential. The biggest difference is that in commercial sales, one is selling the products of a company, while the network marketer is actually selling the company or the system offered by the company. The traditional sales person is looking for consumers of the company's products, while the network marketer is looking not only for the consumer, but for a distributor who will perpetuate the company.

**Betsy Broke:** Is that why the network marketer sees only eight people per month?

**Silver:** Well, she can see more if she so desires and is able to. But a true network marketer knows that she is looking for entrepreneurs not just consumers. It is important that she invests valuable time in building the relationship and the assurance that she will be there to support the new entrepreneur.

**Robbie Rich:** I have had people just invite me to a meeting without full disclosure of what it is about.

**Silver:** While I think meetings are fine for someone who understands already, I think a true entrepreneur will invest in you as a potential entrepreneur and clearly explain the system to you. If they are not confident about explaining the system, then perhaps they should go and learn first and not rely too much on their sponsor or meetings. If you focus too much on making the money and not learn the system properly enough that you can own it yourself and represent it, then you will not be able to make the money you desire.

**Robbie Rich:** So, if I join a network marketing system, what should I do first?

**Silver:** First have a vision. Without a vision you will be groping in the dark. Then study the system fully – all material and discuss with your sponsor any other questions. When you are sold out, then sign up. Set up your home office and set your goals. Have an action plan and implement it. Keep good records and monitor your progress. Stop often to evaluate. Develop you teaching skills and client-care skills so that you can grow your network.

**Robbie Rich**: Would that guarantee me success?

**Silver:** Success is a personal thing. It is not guaranteed to anyone.

# *50*

---

# Are you Self-employed or are you in Business?

*"To carry on a successful business, a man must have imagination."*

Charles M. Schwab

**Robbie Rich:** Earlier when we spoke about acquiring specialised skills, we touched on the issue of self-employment or starting your own business. What if you are a professional and you want to start your own consulting business? What is the best way to go about it?

**Silver:** Well, there is two ways: You can be self-employed or you could start your own business.

**Robbie Rich:** Isn't that the same thing?

**Silver:** No it's not. Unfortunately most people think it is, and they make a mistake of calling self-employment a business. When you are self-employed, all you have done is looked for a different employer, namely, yourself. Unfortunately your situation may be worse than if you had stayed with your previous employer, or actually went and looked for employment elsewhere.

**Robbie Rich:** I don't understand, what do you mean?

**Silver:** You now have to do all other functions of an employer, in addition to doing you actual work.

**Robbie Rich:** No but you get to hire some assistant for administration and office work.

**Silver:** That is true. That is what most self-employed people do.

**Robbie Rich:** Yeah, then you are in business. That is how a business runs!

**Silver:** There is no entrepreneur who would do that. An entrepreneur focuses on revenue producing activities, not revenue consuming activities. If you are self-employed, you are the only one who brings in the revenue that pays for the office administrator, the rent, the telephone bills, etc, and if there is anything left over, you get to pay yourself. Under these circumstances, would a self-employed person take a holiday?

**Robbie Rich:** What would an entrepreneurial medical doctor do?

**Silver:** A business-minded professional is the one who would think of revenue first. She would hire other income-producers first. From the income they are bringing in, based on targets they've agreed to, she would pay them salaries, and have enough left over to pay running costs, including her own salary.

**Robbie Rich:** Oh, I see the difference! A doctor in business hires other doctors. A lawyer in business hires other lawyers. An engineer in business hires other engineers. There are more income producers and few income consumers. One or two administrators, but five or more revenue producers. This way, they can each even afford to go on holiday without worrying about closing the business down!

**Silver:** Exactly. The funny thing is most people who end up in a self-employment situation, actually hate the paperwork that goes with running a business. A doctor would much rather be a doctor than an administrator.

**Robbie Rich:** But if they had a business model they could hire a business manager who would ensure the marketing, the accounting, and other administrative issues, and still be able to have fun doing what they love.

**Silver:** So the model that you use is the key difference.

# *51*

---

# **The Power of Good Contacts**

*"Aim for success, not perfection. Never give up your right to be wrong, because then you will lose the ability to learn new things and move forward with your life."*
Dr. David M. Burns

Never underestimate the value of good contacts. Having a powerful contact list can make the difference between success and failure, happiness and frustration. The most successful people, including doctors, writers and artists as well as businesspeople, are constantly improving the work they do by relying on the help and advice of others.

Here, as promised previously, we talk about networking. What is the difference between networking and selling? Mark H. McCormack, in his book: "*Never Wrestle with a Pig*", writes: "Don't make the mistake of networking with people you want to do business with. That's not networking; that's selling. The best people to keep in touch with are the ones with whom you are already doing business - namely your customers, clients, and suppliers. If you make it a point to stay in touch with customers and clients about matters that concern them, it's almost inevitable that over time they will be curious about matters that concern you. They'll volunteer to help you. That is the essence of effective networking: People helping you out whether or not there's anything in it for them."

Now wouldn't we all love to have people helping us, whether or not there's something in it for them? With due respect to McCormack, I think you need to differentiate between customer relations management (CRM) and networking. I think networking is much broader than customer relations management and selling.

Michael Masterson, author of *Automatic Wealth* –

*The Six steps to financial independence*, and creator of the *Early To Rise* (ETR)[24] e-zine suggests that you think about it this way: whatever success you have had so far -- large or small -- can be furthered by supporting your ambitions with a dozen or so smart and helpful people you can count on. So, today, you re going to promise yourself that you will make your future life richer (in every sense) and also easier by building or continuing to build a network. That's today's resolution.

We are talking, essentially, about people who have things you lack (e.g., money, power, knowledge, etc.). When you need what they have, they will be just a phone call or e-mail away.

First, consider this question: If you could be on a first-name basis with anyone in your trade or your industry, who would it be? Whose power or position would you most like to gain access to? Who among all the people you know of could

---

[24] www.earlytorise.com

have the most positive impact on your future?

Make a list of all the people who could give your career a real boost. It could include someone who runs a successful business similar to yours or someone in a completely unrelated field who has qualities or skills you'd like to have yourself.

You're going to send a short note to one or two of the people on your list every month from now on. And you're going to continue to add to your list.

Start, today, with the name at the top of your list. Think about something this person has done that you admire. It may be a product he has recently developed. It may be the standard of service he sets. It may be something he has written or accomplished or an award he has won. Anything you genuinely admire. On some very nice, dignified stationery, you're going to write him a handwritten note expressing your feelings. Don't flatter. Be direct and complimentary. I did say handwritten, not e-mail. There is more e-mail today than the good old handwritten and posted notes. Your e-mail will get deleted by the secretary before it is read by your intended recipient. A card might get a chance of being displayed on their desk, and might actually get a response.

End with some sort of effort to establish contact. You might ask his opinion on a certain matter, suggest a possible joint venture, or simply request a personal interview. You can, for example, say something like this: "I know you are a very busy person -- but if you ever have a spare half-hour, I'd love the chance to get some advice from you on my own career." Insert your business card and post it. Yes, go to the post office and buy a stamp – you know, the one you lick and paste?

(About that business card, make sure it is not just a card with your name and contact details on it. If your company name does not tell what business you are in, make sure that the business card has a few bulleted points of some of your services.)

Don't expect to get a positive answer from every note you write, but do expect to get some response. If you commit yourself to this program, you will eventually be on a first-name basis with a handful of very influential people.

Set realistic goals. Promise yourself that you will make at least one contact per month (12 for the year) -- and keep at it until you have a list of 12 good souls you can rely on.

You can start with a mixed list of people -- some who can help you with your wealth-building goals, some who can help you become healthier or more social or wiser. Eventually, you may have separate lists for separate endeavours. Commit to one new contact a month. Before you know it, your life will change.

# 52

---

## The Bold Or the Beautiful?

*"In my opinion, it is imperative that our school systems begin teaching financial education as soon as possible. Learning how to manage and invest money is certainly as important as learning how to dissect a frog."*

Robert Kiyosaki

**Silver:** If you are faced with an apparent opportunity of a lifetime; it calls for an investment of your entire life savings, and then some. If it works, you could be rich, but if it fails, you could be bankrupt. There are no guarantees. What would you do? Would you be the bold, or the beautiful? The reckless or the sensible?

**Betsy Broke:** I would most certainly throw all

caution to the wind and be bold. I mean, life has never given any guarantees anyway!

**Robbie Rich:** I think I would be beautiful. It is important to be sensible. There is no point acting irresponsibly and then suffering the consequences for a long time.

**Betsy Broke:** Well look at where sensibility has brought us. We've been slaving away sensibly for the rest of our lives, and if we don't do something radical we might end up bankrupt anyway!

**Robbie Rich:** But with this financial education, we now have a chance to take reasonable chances by being able to calculate the risk and assess whether we can afford the risk or not.

**Betsy Broke:** Yeah but you forgot the one side of this proposition.

**Robbie Rich:** Which is what?

**Betsy Broke:** If this works we could be rich! Why can't you focus only on the possibility of it working out and forget the downside?

**Robbie Rich:** I don't think you should forget the downside. I think you should look at the whole picture, and make an informed decision.

**Betsy Broke:** The whole picture is this: If it works you could be rich. If it fails you could be bankrupt. How can you average that? It is either one or the other. What you are proposing is not to get involved. You are proposing to maintain the status quo. How does that propel us anywhere?

**Robbie Rich:** Perhaps that's what I am proposing. But all I am saying is consider how far you have come. How hard you have worked to gather up all you have right now; if you lose it all, do you still have the strength and the opportunities to start afresh and build it all up again?

**Betsy Broke:** But you could be rich and never have to do it again; so, be bold!

**Robbie Rich:** Or you could be broke and have to do it again, what then?

**Betsy Broke:** Look, doing it over again may not be as arduous as doing it for the first time. All that experience may come to fruition. I say be bold and take your chances. You live once!

**Robbie Rich:** Don't forget that bankruptcy may mean bad credit rating and therefore make it impossible to get a loan to leverage your success.

**Betsy Broke:** Then the opportunity will pass you by…

**Robbie Rich:** Maybe it is disaster that is passing me by … Perhaps it is your reckless attitude that has gotten us into so much debt …

**Betsy Broke:** Perhaps it is your cautionary attitude that has let opportunities pass us by …

\*\*\*

**Silver:** Perhaps we could find a solution to your dilemma …

**Betsy Broke:** How on earth are we going to do that … there seems to be no middle ground between us …

**Silver:** You could continue to chew each other out, or you could decide to work together. Stop playing as individuals and experience the power of teamwork.

**Robbie Rich:** Yeah, she takes the risk and I bear the consequences!

**Betsy Broke:** Oh I like that. I take the risk with my resources. You protect us with yours. If I win, or when I win, we share the plunder.

**Robbie Rich:** And when you lose I carry the load
…

**Betsy Broke:** At least we won't be homeless!

Well what do you think? To be bold, or to be beautiful?

Perhaps in *Another Conversation with Robbie Rich and Betsy Broke* …

Ciao!

## Reader Comments:

> *Hello, Thank you so much for your inspirational articles which appear in the Silver Line. They have made a difference, but you know what, I have a problem in taking risks, I really want to get into the business industry but am afraid it may not turn up to be successful. What can I do? It is difficult to get a loan from [lending institutions] and don't know where else I can get the money. LI.*

# 53

---

# Decisions, A Pathway To Power

*"All the breaks you need in life wait within your imagination. Imagination is the workshop of your mind, capable of turning mind energy into accomplishment and wealth."*
Napoleon Hill.

Procrastination is not only a thief of time, but of dreams and visions as well. The paralysis of analysis is a disease that accompanies procrastination. Fear is a crowning glory of the doubtful and sluggards. And the road to hell is paved with good intentions.

"It is in your moment of decision that your destiny is shaped", says Anthony Robbins.

**Betsy Broke:** Let's face it today, is it mind power or action power. What really gets things going in one's life?

**Robbie Rich:** I think it is mind power. Imagine what the power of fear can do in your life. It literally paralyses you. You can be so afraid that you don't do anything.

**Betsy Broke:** But if I have overcome the fear, then it is my actions, doing something that will get me somewhere, not just sitting around and using mind power.

**Robbie Rich:** Aimless actions will get you nowhere. Too many people are very busy, but they are accomplishing nothing, because they have not set specific goals. So decisions, is really the pathway to power!

**Betsy Broke:** I have taken decisions before but very often have failed to carry them out. So what's the use?

**Robbie Rich:** What sabotaged your decisions? What made you stray from your path?

**Betsy Broke:** I don't know. I just wake up one day and realise that I am way off course. I have strayed into the bushes and I am right where I started. How do I resolve this straying business?

**Silver:** The solution is in the sixth step. Many of us ignore the sixth step or we get bored with it. But power lies in the sixth step.

**Betsy Broke:** The sixth step of what? What are you talking about?

**Silver:** Napoleon Hill writes a six-step approach to getting wealthy in "*Think and Grow Rich*", that states:

1. Determine the exact amount of money that you desire. It is not sufficient to simply say "I want plenty of money". Be definite as to the amount.

2. Determine exactly what you intend to give in return for what you desire. Yes, you must give something!

3. Establish a definite date when you intend to possess your desire.

4. Create a definite plan for carrying out your desire and begin at once, whether you are ready or not, to put this plan into action.

5. Write a clear, concise statement of all four

points above.

6. Finally, read your written statement aloud, twice daily. Rehearse until your subconscious is converted.

**Betsy Broke:** But what's the use of repeating something to yourself everyday?

**Silver:** The conversion of your subconscious mind. There are things you repeat to yourself everyday anyway; your negative statements, your complaints, and your self-criticism. And those are the things that get fulfilled in your life because you have a momentum of negativity. The trouble is, you have done them so much that they are now your second nature. You are now doing them without (consciously) thinking. The idea of deliberately repeating your desired goals to yourself everyday is so that they can become your second nature, and you can start doing them without thinking. That is the power of the mind! Success is a personal thing. You must build a personal momentum of the success energy. Repetition, out loud, creates a feedback loop.

**Betsy Broke:** What do you mean by a feedback

loop?

**Silver:** The words are from yourself to yourself. They come from your mouth into your own ears. That is the self-created feedback loop. You have previously listened to and repeated the words and beliefs of others. It is time you practiced the sixth step daily.

## *Reader Comments*

Hi, I read your article in the newspaper about mentoring. I like the idea of forming a mastermind group where people can share ideas and help each other. I think it is a good idea and I would certainly be interested in joining the group. Regards, B.D.

# 54

---

# We Become What We Think About

*"There is something I do not know, the knowing of which could change everything."*

Werner Erhard.

In one of the earliest audio recordings that launched the spoken word industry entitled "The Strangest secret", Earl Nightingale, dubbed the dean of personal development, says one of the problems that people face today is that people simply don't think. This problem is evident in the way people just conform and do things that they have done for years without knowing exactly why they are doing them.

In his book, *Conversations with God,* Walsch deals with this issue of conformity by talking about the denial syndrome. We see how things are but we deny the truth and hold on to some non-existent "ideal", and therefore are unable to solve our problems.

Walsch asks several questions that address the status quo and the desire to change:

"What is your objective in this life? Do you want to live a life of peace, joy, and love? Then observe that violence does not work.

Do you want to live a life of good health and great longevity? Then observe that consuming dead flesh of animals that have been force fed chemicals; smoking known carcinogens, and drinking volumes of nerve-deadening, brain-frying liquids does not work.

Do you want to raise your offspring free of violence and rage? Then realize that putting them directly in front of vivid depictions of violence and rage for years does not work."

In his book, *Automatic Wealth*, Michael

Masterson enumerates six steps to financial independence, and the very first one has to do with facing the facts. Most people are caught up in the thick of thin things. They have not determined their objectives and thus don't even know where they're at in relation to where they say they want to go. So the first step is: *face the facts*.

The second step is: *plan to become wealthy*. Make a plan and follow it. Loral Langemeier, author of *Cash Machine for Life*, says God does not deliver confusion, but he delivers clarity. Get clear about your goals.

The third step is to *develop wealthy habits*. If you have bad money habits it does not matter how lofty your goal is on paper. If you have habits such as impulsive spending and are caught in spiralling debt, you won't make it.

The fourth step is to *radically increase your income*. It is not about reducing your expenses, but it is about increasing your income. It is much easier to do that than to reduce your spending.

Masterson's fifth step is: *get richer while you*

*sleep*. This step refers to developing passive income streams. Systems such as Network marketing, real estate, and great businesses, including the productive use of the Internet, rather than addiction to social media, are ways to develop passive income streams. And finally, the sixth step is: *retire early!* This of course is a natural progression if you followed the other six steps. Now, who will take that first step of facing the facts?

# *55*

---

## FEAR vs. DESIRE

*"The rights of men are not dependent on the generosity of the state, but upon the hand of God ... ask not what your country can do for you, but what you can do for your country."*

J.F. Kennedy

**Silver:** What is the one thing that can compel you forward in all your endeavours?

**Robbie Rich:** Great Desire!

**Silver:** What is the one thing that can stop you dead in your tracks?

**Betsy Broke:** Fear!

Silver: Dr. J. Murphy, author of *The Power of your*

*Subconscious Mind*, writes: It has been said that people's greatest enemy is fear. Fear is behind failure, sickness, and poor human relations. Millions of people are afraid of the past, the future, old age, insanity, [poverty, wealth], and death. But fear is a thought in your mind. This means that you are afraid of your own thoughts.

**Betsy Broke:** A small child can be paralyzed with fear when a playmate says there is a monster under the bed ...

**Robbie Rich:** But when the parent turns on the light and shows there is no monster, he is freed from fear. **Silver:** The fear in the mind of the child was every bit as real as if there were really a monster there. He was healed of a false thought in his mind. The thing he feared did not exist. In the same way, most of your fears have no reality.

Consider another tale about a young man who asked the great philosopher Socrates how he could get wisdom.

"Come with me," Socrates replied. He took the lad to a river and shoved his head underwater.

He held it there until the boy struggled for air. Then he let him go. Once the boy regained his composure, Socrates asked him, "What did you desire most when your head was under water?"

"I wanted air," the boy told him. Socrates nodded slowly. "When you want wisdom as much as you wanted air when your were immersed in the water, you will receive it."

**Robbie Rich:** In the same way, when your desire for something is greater than your fear of obstacles and whatever else there is to fear, and when you come to a clear-cut decision that there is a way out, then victory and triumph are assured.

**Silver:** Ralph Waldo Emerson, the great nineteenth-century philosopher and poet, said: "Do the thing you are afraid to do, and the death of fear is certain."

Whatever you fear has its solution in the form of your desire. If you are sick, you desire health.

**Robbie Rich:** True. Consider what great victories

have been won by people who faced great tribulations along the way: Civil rights movements have won great victories even after facing severe persecutions, because their desire for freedom far exceeded their fears of tribulations.

**Silver:** Consider what the reverend Martin Luther King Jr. said in that great "I have a dream" speech: "Let us not wallow in the valley of despair. I say to you my friends, that in spite of the difficulties and frustrations of the moment, I still have a dream …"

### *READER COMMENTS*

*Dear Nelson, I enjoyed reading your article "Conquer Fear" (Fear vs Desire) in the Botswana Guardian of 15th July 2005. Thank you for being a source of encouragement as I have very big dreams to accomplish. I am a Director of a young/emerging company and have business/success dreams, which I know are not too big for God.*

*1. I would appreciate the full speech of "I have a dream" by Martin Luther King Jr. Could you please e-mail it to me.*

*2. What were the circumstances under which John F Kennedy said, "The rights of men are not dependent on the generosity of the state, but upon the hand of God ... ask not what your country can do for you, but what you can do for your country"? If you have the relevant speech, please let me have it. Regards, NN*

# Further Reading

1. The Richest Man in Babylon, George S. Clason
2. Think and Grow Rich, Napoleon Hill
3. Automatic Wealth, Michael Masterson
4. Rich Dad Poor Dad, Robert Kiyosaki
5. Cash Flow Quadrant, Robert Kiyosaki
6. Acres of Diamonds, Russell Conwel
7. As a Man Thinketh, James Allen
8. The Seven Spiritual Laws of Success, Deepak Chopra
9. 10 Secrets for Success and Inner Peace, Wayne W. Dyer
10. Mind Power into the 21st Century, John Kehoe
11. The New Psycho-Cybernetics, Maxwell Maltz
12. Personal Financial Management, Nico Swart
13. I can do it, Louise Hay
14. Screw it, Let's Do it, Richard Branson
15. Conversations with God, book 1, Neale Donald Walsch

# Acknowledgements

There is no denying that all inspiration to even attempt to write a book comes from God through The Mighty I AM Presence. I therefore acknowledge my Holy Christ Self for shepherding all ideas expressed in this book.

Deciding to become a columnist that supplies material of one subject like personal finance is challenging in that you may always wonder what next week would be about. But for eleven years, week in week out, The Silverline column ran and covered more ground than we even imagined we would cover. Thanks indeed to the engagement of the readers who kept sending comments and questions that kept the conversation going.

My gratitude goes to the editors of The Botswana Guardian who kept publishing the Silveline column every week. It was first Outsa Mokone, then Mike Mothibi, then Mpho Dibeela, and finally Joel Konopo. The column was shepherded by other staff members of the Botswana Guardian over those years. It became the longest running column of its kind for the newspaper over those eleven years. It was not retired because we ran out of things to say, but that it just needed to retire at the right time.

Thank you to my family for their continued support for such projects that often take too much time to complete.

My gratitude also goes to the team at Moedi Learning Technologies. I thank my Mastermind group of mentors that continued to encourage me over the years: Lets Sithole and Lerumo Mompoloki Mogobe.

If you have never had the chance to read the Silverline column, this book brings the packaged version of it to your table. Enjoy.

Thank you

Nelson Letshwene

Gaborone, Botswana
September 2019

# About The Author

Nelson Letshwene is a financial planner, and a speaker and writer with over two decade of experience. He has published hundreds of articles in the field of personal development, motivation and personal finance, as well as in the field of faith and spirituality.

He has lived in South Africa, Zimbabwe and Botswana and has travelled internationally. He continues to hold seminars in the field of personal finance, human development, spirituality, and motivation.

Nelson Letshwene's other books are currently available from www.amazon.com

# Other Books By R Nelson Letshwene

 *The Money Field* is like a sports field upon which the game of money is played. In its four quadrants are various players including yourself. Each player's goal is to win. This book gives you the rules, winning strategies and how others play against you. Will you win this game? The money game is life's compulsory game. Everyone who handles money is automatically a player. Time to play and win!

 Seven Essential Money Skills are to be installed, activated, and practiced in order to transform you and your relationship with your money. Learn skills to create multiple streams of income, to save and invest, to protect and build controls, to build long lasting value and to share your bounty with others. Everyone who handles money must have these skills.

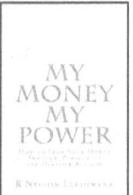 **My Money My Power!** Your money came to you in exchange for your power in the form of skill, talent, idea, or sweat. It remains your responsibility to keep that power. It is easy to lose your power to the commercial system and be a slave to lenders and traders. You only retain your power when you turn your money into investments and assets that produce more income. This book is about leading your money through decisive actions to retain your power.

 **If We Were All #Financially Literate!** This book is a thought stimulator – to get us to think about areas of our financial literacy. You may be good in one but lack in another. Earnings; controls; our psychology of money; debt; savings; investments; assets; etc. Take the journey

**Life Insurance and You!** is not just about the importance and the adequacy of your life insurance cover. Know where to look if you're a beneficiary. Learn the claiming process and help loved ones to get their benefits. Can you afford to be uninsured?

FAITH AND PURPOSE. The question of what faith is has kept truth seekers on the path for centuries. Faith is both Art and Science. It is the process of becoming one with your desires and with the creator. Faith is a force in the universe that can make things happen. Purpose is faith with passion. Take this journey now.

Life unfolds according to the desires you hold through your beliefs. Your Longing Is Your Calling is literally the desires that will drive your life. Life is calling you to live it to the full. The call will keep ringing until it is answered. Desire is a propensity to grow. The Seven Desires explored in this book cover the seven basic rivers that run through every life stream.

What you put your attention on, you compel yourself to become. We fall and rise based on the focus of our attention. There is a sermon that causes preachers to fall, especially if preached with passion. Dare to find out, and change.

# THANK YOU

If you enjoyed reading this book, please feel free to leave me a review, especially if you purchased this through the amazon platform. Reviews help other readers to know the relevance of the book for them and they help authors like me to improve on our work and to know if we are meeting your needs.

Thank you for taking the time to leave a review. Much appreciated.

Thank you

Nelson Letshwene

Nelson Letshwene

nelson@moedi.net / nelslets@gmail.com

www.nelsonletshwene.com

@Nletshwene

#JoinTheMoneyConversation

---

[i] Answers to Money Mathematics:

1. Norman lost $130 altogether made up of the $51 that he gave to the customer, and the $79 he paid for the bike.